MW01194600

Life Everlasting:
The Mystery and the Promise

"With superb storytelling and precise thought, Msgr. Bransfield delivers a beautiful truth in *Life Everlasting*. This is not just another book seeking to dismantle the myths of atheism. It is far more. The reader immediately finds themselves faced with the "dilemma" of our mortality and the natural life questions that accompany it. Msgr. Bransfield proves to be a gifted and sage guide as he walks the reader through philosophical canyons and over theological mountains, offering numerous insights and fresh reflections along the way. This book not only reminds us of life's origin, but its purpose, its meaning, and its goal. I look forward to re-reading this book . . . it will help countless souls navigate the often painful waters of life (and death)."

— *Mark Hart, Executive Vice President, Life Teen International,*
and best-selling Catholic author, speaker, and radio host

Life
EVERLASTING

Life
EVERLASTING

The Mystery and the Promise

J. Brian Bransfield

With a Foreword by
Seán Cardinal O'Malley, O.F.M. Cap.

Pauline
BOOKS & MEDIA

Boston

Library of Congress Cataloging-in-Publication Data

Bransfield, J. Brian.
  Life everlasting : the mystery and the promise / J. Brian Bransfield.
    pages cm
  ISBN 978-0-8198-4580-1 (pbk.) -- ISBN 0-8198-4580-9 (pbk.)
  1. Eschatology. 2. Death--Religious aspects--Catholic Church. 3. Future life--Catholic Church. I. Title.
  BT821.3.B73 2015
  236'.2--dc23

                          2015001223

Cover design by Rosana Usselmann

Cover photo istockphoto.com/© theevening

Published by Pauline Books & Media, 50 Saint Pauls Avenue, Boston, MA 02130–3491

Printed in the U.S.A.

www.pauline.org

Pauline Books & Media is the publishing house of the Daughters of St. Paul, an international congregation of women religious serving the Church with the communications media.

1 2 3 4 5 6 7 8 9   19 18 17 16 15

For
Reverend Monsignor Ronny E. Jenkins, S.T.L., J.C.D.

*"When they heard
of the resurrection of the dead,
some scoffed, but others said,
'We should like to hear you on this some other time.'"*

— ACTS OF THE APOSTLES 17:32

—

Contents

Foreword

One of my favorite biblical images of Jesus is that of the Good Shepherd. He comes to gather the scattered and to seek out the lost sheep with great care, compassion, and mercy. The shepherd's staff that Jesus uses to gather the scattered is the cross. It is the power of the cross that gathers us into one. Yet this gathering requires the shepherd to lay down his life in Jerusalem.

Jesus' last stop in his journey toward his death and resurrection was Bethany, a small village that was home to the siblings Martha, Mary, and Lazarus. It was an oasis of friendship, hospitality, and peace for Jesus. It was where he went when he wanted to be surrounded by the love of his friends. It is no surprise that Jesus made this his last stop before proceeding to his suffering and death in Jerusalem. Bethany prepared Jesus for Jerusalem.

We all need "Bethanys" in our lives—especially when we face difficult decisions, trials, oppositions, suffering, and death. In the prayerful atmosphere of Bethany we can deepen our sense of vocation and our friendship with the Lord, who calls us to eternal life with him. If we have not visited Bethany, we will never survive Jerusalem. I am so grateful to Reverend Monsignor J. Brian Bransfield for the gift of this book, *Life Everlasting: The Mystery and the Promise*. It is a Bethany for us in that it helps us to grapple with the real questions of death and pain in the light of the Lord's promise of hope and of eternal life.

In the early chapters of the book, Monsignor Bransfield takes us through his personal experiences as a boy attending his first wake, and the upheaval of his life when his mother died suddenly. He was only twelve years old at the time. Yet these experiences of death allowed him, at a young age, to ask the big questions of life. They have allowed him to reflect deeply in order to share the wisdom that is contained within this profoundly moving volume.

My hope is that this book will be like a visit to Bethany for us, allowing us to grow in our awareness of Christ's presence in our lives—especially during times of suffering and pain—so that when we inevitably encounter them, we will rest firmly in the hope that is ours in Christ Jesus, who is the Way, the Truth, and the Life. Psalm 126 reminds us that God transforms our tears into laughter and our sorrow into joy. I pray that through this book, we may visit Bethany, surrounded by Christ's friendship and transformed by his healing love.

✠ Seán Cardinal O'Malley, O.F.M. Cap.
Archbishop of Boston

Acknowledgments

The opening chapter of this book begins with the events on an afternoon in August 1977, in a small room, in a house on Lyceum Avenue in Philadelphia. The concluding chapter ends in that same small room, sixteen years later, in October 1993. The actual events described are meant to serve as both the launching pad and the landing gear, to help the reader explore the teaching of the Church on the mystery of death, eternal life, and the four last things.

Though the events of those two days are etched in my memory, these chapters would likely never have been written without a request I received from my editor at Pauline Books & Media in Boston, Massachusetts, on the Feast of Our Lady of Guadalupe, December 12, 2012. Sister kindly requested that I consider writing a book on the mystery of death, eternal life, and the four last things. Before that day I had never thought of doing so. After writing this book, I cannot imagine *not* having done so.

I am, therefore, deeply grateful to the team at Pauline Books & Media for their considerable expertise in all the details of publication that have brought this work to completion. In particular, I am thankful to Sr. Sean Mayer, FSP; Sr. Marianne Lorraine Trouvé, FSP; Sr. Donna Giaimo, FSP; Mrs. Cathy Knipper; Ms. Vanessa Reese; Ms. Kaelin Corina; and Mr. Brad McCracken.

Finally, I am most grateful to the Most Reverend Charles J. Chaput, O.F.M., Cap., the Archbishop of my home archdiocese of Philadelphia, for his encouragement and support; and to Cardinal Seán O'Malley, O.F.M. Cap., for the thoughtful and moving foreword of this work.

Introduction

*"Jesus says Yes to his Father's creation
and goes in search of all beings lost in the world maze,
in order to bring them home."* [1]

—HANS URS VON BALTHASAR

At every death one can find the thread or clue for the journey to discover its meaning. That journey takes us along the way of the teaching of the Church on the mystery of eternal life and the four last things. In this book we will journey together, examining the mysteries of salvation as they relate to human death and eternal life with God. As we do, we take as our principal method what Cardinal Pierre de Bérulle, the sixteenth-century French mystic, referred to

---

1. Hans Urs von Balthasar, *Theodrama Theological Dramatic Theory IV: The Action* (San Francisco: Ignatius Press, 1994), 444, cf. 78.

as "the science of salvation."[2] Usually we associate science with the study of biology, chemistry, or physics. But science, in its most basic meaning, refers to an ordered and logical body of knowledge. Science is the study of a series of connections. Catholic theology is a science, the first of the sciences.[3] Catholic theology presents the highest of realities: divine revelation by which God reveals to us knowledge of the mysteries of God's own life. This is why Saint Paul encourages us, "[God] has made known to us the mystery of his will, according to his good pleasure that he set forth in Christ, as a plan for the fullness of time, to gather up all things in him, things in heaven and things on earth" (Eph 1:9–10). Divine revelation assists our own natural reason as we find our way.

Many fine books have identified the steps of the grieving process, and those works are important and helpful. This book does not outline precise steps, but it is also designed to help those who mourn the loss of a friend or loved one. The experience of loss and reflection on eternal life are not two separate topics—they lead into each other. When we meet one, we meet the other. In considering the mystery of eternal life made known through the words and deeds of Jesus we must first consider human death. Through examples of my own experience that served as the basis of crucial clues hiding right in the open, we will follow the thread through one of the oldest mysteries that the human race has faced: the mystery of death and eternal life. Remember, mystery cannot be rushed. Gentleness is the handle by which we open the door of mystery. Therefore, this work devotes time to highlight connections hidden beneath the sacred

---

2. Pierre de Bérulle, *Discourse on the State and the Grandeurs of Jesus* as in *Bérulle and the French School Selected Writings*, The Classics of Western Spirituality (New Jersey: Paulist Press, 1989), 116.

3. Saint Thomas Aquinas, *Summa Theologiae* Ia, q 1, a 5; cf. IIa IIae, q 1, a 5.

words that we have listened to thousands of times at Mass, found in prayers, or have read in the Bible. These words convey the hidden plan of God. Because we frequently hear these words, ideas, and concepts, we may pass over them rather quickly. Here we will slowly pass a magnifying glass over the events that surround death, daily life, reason, and the great truths of faith. We want to dust for prints, follow the thread, examine the clues and, ultimately, like our Lady, treasure these truths in our heart (see Lk 2:19). This is the task of the New Evangelization: to see what is already familiar to us on one level and understand it in a new, exciting, and life-giving way. We can have access to the depths of the mystery through grace, which builds upon effective strategies of Catholic education, meditation, and preaching.

When our loved ones die, we look at the world differently. We look at our faith differently. This book opens up the faith so that it can be seen through tear-filled eyes. Let's not hesitate to step closer to the great mystery of the wonderful works of God.

CHAPTER ONE

Questions and Clues about Death

The long line of people stretched out the front door of the large house, down the steps, and then around the street corner. The people in that long line looked as if they were standing on a slow-moving conveyor belt no one wanted to be on but that, nonetheless, mercilessly inched forward. Many of them had rushed around all day, busy with errands, deadlines, and routine appointments, yet now they were in no hurry to climb the steps of the Fitzpatrick Funeral Home. But, once inside, *they were sure in a hurry to get out*.

I had just turned ten years old and had never been to a "wake" before. There I stood, wearing a suit and tie in the heat of that August afternoon, as my family waited our turn to walk in and pay our respects and condolences to the grieving family. A classmate's father had died after a long battle with cancer. As the line inched forward and I stepped onto the porch, I was aware of an odd feeling in my stomach—not a feeling of being sick, but as if my stomach was trying to fly away. Despite that feeling, I was rather quiet, like everyone else. But during the car ride from our house to the funeral home I had been anything but quiet. I pelted my parents with questions: "What's a wake?" "Is he going to be in a bed?" "Are they going to try to wake him up?"

"No," my mother had replied, "that won't happen."

"If he isn't going to wake up," I responded, "then why call it a wake?" I then tried to compute the words "funeral home." "What's a funeral home?" "Why does a funeral have a home?" "Does a family live there?" Based on what I had heard about "funeral homes," I thought the house would have looked a bit spookier: shutters hanging off their hinges; creaky, cracked floor boards on a dusty porch; and a broken window or two at least. But the house I now stood in front of didn't appear haunted or ghostly. It was the opposite—it seemed *sterile*. No toys littered the manicured lawn. The expansive porch had no furniture and no television blared from the next room. Everything was too clean: overly-polished and seemingly untouched, as if no one lived there. For a funeral home, sterile and bland seemed *worse* than spooky and haunted. Sterile was feeling-less, barren, and . . . *lifeless*.

I had no clue of what to expect as we stood before the large front doors of this muted and antiseptic house. During our car ride my parents had told me that a "wake" was not for the deceased, but for the people who attended. It was their opportunity to see the person for the last time and to express sympathies to his family. "*See* the person?" I asked. "But they're dead. Why are they in a house?" I thought dead people were only in cemeteries. My mother explained that this was before the body was taken to the cemetery. The person's body would be here and it would also be at the funeral. It was an opportunity to say a final goodbye. I could not get my mind around the body being there. Saying "goodbye" sounded strange to me as well, since a dead person cannot hear. I said, "Why say goodbye now?" "Why didn't people say goodbye while he was alive?" My mom told me, again, that it was more for the family. The weird feeling in my stomach increased as we inched closer to the house. My questions, though many, did not simply come from my curiosity. I was dimly aware that my questions arose more from a desire to delay the trip than from pure inquisitiveness.

My questions vanished as we passed through the large front doors of the imposing house. I braced myself and looked. I felt relieved when I realized we had simply stepped into a hallway. The body was not in sight. I could see that the line turned around a corner of the hallway. It wasn't so bad. My apprehension lessened a bit. I still felt some suspense, wondering what I would see. My father pointed out to me the collection of holy cards on the side table, handed me one, and told me to put it in my pocket. He showed me how to sign the guest book that rested on a shiny podium. Feeling important as I signed my name, I also tried to see my reflection in the polished podium.

Then it was our turn; we stepped forward and turned the corner. And I *looked*. As I did, that slow conveyor belt I had been on ground to a halt. My legs stopped inching forward. My stomach went solid. I forgot to swallow. My breath disappeared and hid in my lungs. I was no more than three-feet away from a highly-polished mahogany coffin with white-satin pillow lining all around and the lid propped wide open. The coffin seemed densely massive to me. My friend's father was lying inside wearing a blue pinstripe suit. Though his eyes were closed, he was wearing eyeglasses. At first he seemed to be sleeping, but I noticed something else, something "caky," unusual, and rigid about his skin. His lips seemed unnatural and waxy, like they were made of thin, pink plastic. His clay-colored hands were folded stiffly over his waist with a rosary intertwined in his taut fingers. Worst of all he didn't *move*. The man in the coffin had no breath; *his* chest didn't rise and fall. As I looked down from his chest, I saw he wasn't actually holding the rosary beads. They were instead loosely draped over the fingers. The fingers didn't move at all, not even slightly.

No words could have prepared me for that scene. All I could do was stare as my mouth gaped open. As I stood there my next thought was: "Why are there pillows lining the coffin?" My mom had told me earlier that a dead person cannot feel anything. Why were cushions there if he couldn't feel anything?

Then I saw a medium-sized wooden crucifix propped up in the corner of the coffin, resting against the open lid. I had only seen crucifixes in three places. First, I had seen the crucifix hanging on a nail in the wall—at church, in people's homes, or on the wall of my classroom at school. Second, I had also seen people wearing the crucifix around their necks as jewelry. Third, I had a small crucifix on the nightstand by my bed. Like most ten-years-olds, I had a very concrete thinking style. I was surprised to see the crucifix in the coffin. Of all the unknown things I feared seeing in the funeral home, I had not expected to see a crucifix. Its *unexpectedness* made it *stand out* all the more to me. The crucifix not only caught my attention, but it also formed a sort of nucleus to all that was going on. I recall asking later that afternoon: "Why was a crucifix propped up in the corner of the coffin?" My mother had explained that when they closed the coffin they would take out the crucifix and affix it to the top of the coffin.

I can still see that image of the wooden crucifix strongly contrasted against the white pillow and satin background. In fact, over the years, when I have gone to a funeral home in the course of my priestly ministry, the image of the crucifix in the corner is the first image that comes to my mind's eye. It is etched in my memory. It was the unexpected center of all else. I can still sense the abiding lesson that only hope can teach: the sign of the ultimate gift and victory of Christ was present where I had not expected to see it. I thought God was only at work if he acted in a big way—if the dead man came back to life. But, despite my expectation, God was somehow already unpredictably at work even here in this difficult, unexplored place from which I wanted to escape.

Finally, I felt my father's large hand on my small back moving me gently forward. I shuffled along the side of the open coffin and gazed in. I still remember the dark suit contrasted against the white pillow lining, and his long legs stretched to the opposite end of the coffin. The image of his legs would come back in numerous nightmares later that night. Then I saw my mother reach and touch the dead man's hand as she said a prayer. *I was still within reach.* I looked up and my mother nodded. *I wanted to and I didn't want to at the same time.* I reached out my small hand and touched the dead man's hand. It felt cold, coarse, and hard. I yanked my hand back quickly. I was shocked at how dense and rubbery the skin felt. It was as if my touch came directly back to me. Years later I would read Nicholas Wolterstorff's memoir on the death of his son. Wolterstorff describes his first reaction on touching the lifeless body of his son: "Death, I knew, was cold. And death was still. But nobody had mentioned that all the softness went out."[1] I was not expecting skin to feel that way.

After we greeted the family, we stepped back on the invisible conveyor belt and moved quickly out the rear door of the funeral home. I was glad to be outside in the warm sunshine again. The breath ran out of my lungs. My legs moved quickly. So did my questions . . . especially about that touch.

That summer afternoon was not to be my final visit to a funeral home. In fact, in the space of the next twenty-seven months, between the ages of ten to twelve, I would return no less than four separate times. The next time was after the death of my grandfather, then of the pastor of our parish, then for the tragic death of a ten-year-old friend, and, finally and worst of all, for my mother. . . .

---

1. Nicholas Wolterstorff, *Lament for a Son* (Michigan: Eerdmans Press, 1987), 8.

For the average seventh grader, lunch is not a meal but a race. The goal is simple: to be the "first one done." In 1979, as an average seventh grader, I was always among the semi-finalists for being the "first one done."

The logic was simple. Morning classes at Immaculate Heart of Mary Elementary School ended precisely at 11:45 AM Every school day, from 11:30 to 11:45 AM, I watched the large clock on our classroom wall like a race-car driver revving his engine as he monitors the countdown. This was before the days of in-school lunches. Since our school had no cafeteria, we each brought our lunches in a small brown paper bag. We ate at our desks, the same desks we sat in for math, English, and spelling class. At 11:45 we stowed away our books and each row of students, when called, went to the back of the room to retrieve his or her lunch bag. We said grace before meals together . . . and then the race was on.

Why the race? After each student had finished eating, he or she was allowed to go to the large schoolyard. That meant uninterrupted fun—the longer, the better. Who had time to eat when we could flip baseball cards, shoot marbles, and pal around with friends?

Monday, November 19, 1979, was a school day like any other. After my row was called, I grabbed my brown paper lunch bag and began munching the ham sandwich and potato chips. On the outside of the lunch bag I momentarily noticed my name, written in black magic marker in my mother's unmistakably neat handwriting. When she prepared lunches a few days in advance she always wrote my name on the outside of the bag. I thought I'd never be able to write like her, in such a precise and predictable way. Her beautiful script, which also graced my test papers and homework, was the same even on the countless grocery lists I held for her as we shopped. Little did I know, as I looked at that paper bag, that this would be the last time my mother would ever write my name.

Every schoolyard has its games and its rules. Sometimes the games, set by the students, and the rules, set by the teachers, collide. By far, the most popular game in November 1979 in our schoolyard was jailbreak. The boys would split into two groups. One group, the "robbers," would run, while the other group, the "police" tried to catch them and put them in jail. Someone had to guard the jail, though, because if even one as-yet-uncaught robber touched the jail and yelled "Free," then all the robbers went free. Of course, the running involved in jailbreak was against the rules. The game required an extra level of skill, for while the robbers tried to evade the police, both police and robbers tried to avoid the omnipresent lunch mothers. But with 800 children milling around, the schoolyard became a large maze with an ever-shifting network of twists and turns amid the crowd: a group of girls talking; another group jumping rope, fourth graders flipping cards nearby, and games of catch popping up here and there. In a game of jailbreak, runners could lose themselves in many places.

And so, I was on the run. As I scooted close to the school doors near the convent, my teacher called me over. My stomach dropped. I had been caught for running. This would mean my first detention. To my knowledge no Bransfield had ever had a detention. What would Mom and Dad say? But suddenly I wondered why my *teacher*, Mrs. Carroll, was in the schoolyard. Recess had just begun. Lunch mothers were supposed to roam the schoolyard, not teachers. And why was Mrs. Carroll calling me *into* the building, not to the infamous "line" where offenders had to stand until lunch ended? Obediently I climbed the school stairs. Mrs. Carroll led me into the convent, where my aunt, a Sister of St. Joseph, was waiting for me. I thought: *All this for running in the schoolyard?* It seemed a lot of trouble for a first-time offender.

Then my aunt led me into the convent and told me in simple terms that my mother, who had been in the hospital for tests but was due home shortly, had taken a turn for the worse. I still remember my aunt's exact words: "She's not too hot." My aunt was very close to me and knew me well. She could be informal. I think, given the news she had to convey, she had to be informal. No one wants to tell a twelve-year-old that his mother is dying.

Because my mother had been having severe chest pains, the doctor had admitted her to the hospital for further tests. With my father, brother, and sisters, I went every night to visit her in the hospital. Each visit, my ears caught only the reference to when my mother would be home: "a few days." After we went home each night we would speak with her on the phone.

She had been moved to a step-down unit and was ready to be discharged: ready to come home, to make ham sandwiches, to continue writing my name on the brown lunch bags, to write the shopping list. She was ready to leave the hospital, to come home and be my mom again.

But as I was to learn later, something happened in the middle of the night. My mother suffered a massive heart attack. Everything changed. The hospital had immediately called my father and told him. They weren't sure how severe it was, so my brother and I went to school not knowing things had taken a turn. Then, mid-morning the doctor told my father: "You had better bring the whole family in. It doesn't look like she'll make it."

So now I was standing in the convent with my aunt. "Well, your Mom . . . she's not too hot. She's not doing well."

My body knew what those words meant before my mind did. I still cringe when I think of them. My first thought was: *That's impossible*. I had just seen her the night before when the whole family had visited her. She was fine. She was coming home.

My father came to the convent to pick me up. As we walked through the now empty schoolyard, my thoughts came together like a mathematical equation. We had just been with my mom in the hospital last night. Now my brother and I were with Dad, in the middle of a workday. *We had just visited my mom in the hospital last night.* We can go again tonight. *Unless . . .* Too many pieces were falling into place for my young mind, and they were all pointing in the same direction.

When we arrived at the hospital, I walked into the intensive care unit and saw Mom through the large glass window, all hooked up, tubes everywhere, eyes rolled back. Yet she knew. *She knew I was there.* I heard her groan aloud when I walked into the room, as her eyes rolled back further.

Mom died at 3:00 PM. Only three hours earlier I had been playing a game in a schoolyard. Only three hours earlier my single greatest "worry" was getting caught breaking the rule against running in the schoolyard. Now, I had come face-to-face with one of the harshest and most unforgiving rules of life: death.[2] I was colliding with the hard lesson that life has rules, and one of these is death. On most school days at 3:00 PM, I'd burst through the front door and smell my mother's meatballs already simmering as she prepared dinner. On this weekday at 3:00 PM, I was standing in an intensive care unit as the world began to disappear. I suddenly felt stranded and confused, deep in a narrow, tangled, and empty maze of death that had no way out, so I felt lost and adrift. I wanted someone to burst in and yell, "Free!" and release me from this terrible sentence. At twelve years old, I thought my mom would live forever. The daily routine of life that made sense to me had been swept away, never to return. Although

---

2. Donna Tartt summarizes with incisive clarity the significance of the impact of the death of a parent on a young child. See her, *The Goldfinch* (New York: Little, Brown and Company, 2013), 7; see also Malcolm Gladwell, *David and Goliath: Underdogs, Misfits, and the Art of Battling Giants* (New York: Little, Brown, and Company, 2013), 140.

many generous and kind people helped me, I still didn't know where to turn. Most of all, I wanted God to fix things. I wanted him to make it all go away—as if my mom had never died—or somehow reverse all the events of this terrible day. I wanted God to do something big.

But, as the great saints remind us, God often chooses to work in small ways—not *despite* his greatness, but precisely *because of it*. In our pride we take notice of the big things, and we want more of them. But our souls notice the small things and *love* them. Sometimes we can get so wrapped up in ourselves, in our pride, that we demand the big things. When our loved ones die, we look at the world differently. We look at our faith differently. This book opens up the faith so that it can be seen through tear-filled eyes. Let's not hesitate to step closer to the great mystery of the wonderful works of God. Saint Gregory the Great says that the soul is very important, and to nourish it we must seek out the small things that God places in our path to lead us to himself. In fact, Saint Gregory explains that there is a small string or thread *in the human soul*. When we find that thread in our soul, we are invited to follow it. Small things are often fragile. Saint Gregory emphasizes that we must be careful lest we overstrain this thread and it snaps.[3]

Threads are small, but we tend to notice them when they are lying on the floor or hanging from our clothes. Threads have a long history. In Olde English and Middle English the word for "thread" is "clew." A "clew" is a large spool or ball of strong thread, the end of which one ties to a firm fixture so as to venture forward into strange, unfamiliar places. The thread is a "clew" that points out and guides us as we find our way safely through dark and unknown places. In fact, we derive our contemporary word "clue" from the Olde English

---

3. See Saint Gregory the Great, *Pastoral Care* (New Jersey: Paulist Press, 1950), Part III, Ch., 39, page 231.

"clew." A clue is a sturdy landmark that leads us through a puzzling investigation so that we find the truth.

In 1979 I went from being an average, carefree seventh grader to a boy stuck in the narrow, confined, and lonely maze of loss and confusion. There I came upon a thread. In this book I hope to help the reader to recognize and find the thread of eternal life even amid the pain of death, to point out the clues of eternal life in the midst of death's shifting maze. Hans Urs von Balthasar, the eminent Swiss theologian, uses the image of the maze to describe our painful earthly plight. He said that the Lord Jesus goes *into* the maze in search of us in order to bring us home. Jesus is the living Thread, *he* is the One who breaks the bars of the prison of death and frees us. He, the *living* Witness at the heart of his Church, is the One who writes our name in the book of *life*. He is at the center of these pages.

CHAPTER TWO

The Painful "No More"

The pain behind the questions

We pull back and move quickly past death, but its questions linger and remain with us. However many questions I had asked in the car on the way to my first wake, I had twice as many on the way home. "Why was he wearing a suit?" "Why was he wearing glasses?" "Does his body stay in their house all night tonight, and, if so, do kids live in that house?"

More than three decades later, I have to ask another question: "What was behind my many questions about death?" All of the very specific questions I asked that day only scratched the surface of one of the oldest and deepest questions to haunt the human race: What happens to us when we die? Superficial as my questions were, they were based in deep alarm. My persistent curiosity came from some deep place. Children think they will live forever, and that their parents will live forever. That warm August afternoon in 1977 was the first time this basic premise was put into question for me. And so, I was trying to figure out death.

What was behind my many questions? Simply this: I was extremely worried because if he had died, then the people around me could die. If the people around me could die, then I could die. If he had to lie there in the funeral home, then so, too, one day, would the people I loved. And one day I would also have to lie there. One day the bodies of the people I loved would not move. One day their bodies would feel like that. And, one day, so would mine.

Walking through the doors of that funeral home was like walking through a mysterious portal into a maze, as if I had been dropped—alone and for the first time—into the middle of a confusing and shifting labyrinth. In that banal and narrow corridor, I could see no exit signs, doors, or windows. My rapid-fire questions spilled out of my troubled and panicked search for a way back or out, but certainly not forward. I wanted to lose this terrible knowledge I now had. It was as if I somehow knew no answer could allow me to unlearn what I had just seen. I wanted to forget it, but could not.

Yet, for all of the turmoil the visit raised for me, something happened in that moment when I saw my mother touch the dead man's hand. When I, still within reach, looked up wordlessly to her and she nodded, something more happened. When I reached in and touched his hand and felt that all the softness had gone out, something of the reality of death hit home. This troublesome fact has tied people in knots in every age: every human person eventually dies. For as long as we have known this common fact, we have never gotten used to it. Yet, at the same time, I had seen the unexpected presence of the crucifix. These two unexpected moments stood out for me that day and still do today. One spoke to the decisive hardness of death, and the other to the faithful, abiding sign of the ultimate victory of Christ. The two moments did not occur in sequence as much as they *converged*. It was as if the two moments dueled with one another, and, in their contest, I discovered a deeper meaning that always lurks just beyond the surface of life: the thread at the threshold of death-life. The touch and the crucifix became the longitude and latitude of my experience that afternoon, and at their intersection I found a thread. For all of the confusion, I tugged on that thread and felt something firm and secure. I simply couldn't let go of it. It has taken me many years to learn that the thread was more than a thread. It was a clue.

My questions were important. They were my feeble and fearful way of holding on to the thread. And so, what was behind my many questions? What did the thread feel like? Quite simply, my pain was behind my questions. Pain is most likely behind your questions about death as well. The thread I picked up that day in the funeral home when I reached across and touched the hand of the corpse was pain; yet, in the preceding moment I saw the crucifix, and that symbol of faith took on a much deeper meaning for me, a meaning I could not yet explain. That is what the thread looked like to me that day and for many years after.

Feeling the pain death leaves behind

New obituaries appear in the media every few hours. Every day, young people learn about the difficult reality of death for the first time. Though thousands stumble upon it for the first time hourly, the bitterness of death is nothing new. Over the centuries, many people have held the frayed, small end of the cruel thread I held that day. When the prophet Isaiah tells the mortally ill Hezekiah that he will soon die, Hezekiah prays and weeps bitterly (see 2 Kgs 20:1–3). So too, the psalmist rues the time when he will pass away forever (see Ps 49:9). Job tells us that for those who die, "they return no more to their houses, nor do their places know them any more" (Job 7:10). Jeremiah tells us that the *no more* brought about by death, especially of a child, is inconsolable: "Rachel is weeping for her children; she refuses to be comforted for her children, because they are no more" (Jer 31:15). Worse still, the psalmist says that the dead are long forgotten (see Ps 143:3). Death shamelessly cheats. It seems to win every time. No one can quarantine this fatal flaw. It always claims the eventual, terrible last word. The riddle that plagued the psalmist now disturbed me as well: "Who can live and never see death? Who can escape the power of Sheol?" (Ps 89:49). At age ten, I had stumbled up close to the taboo of death for the first time. The words of the psalmist, "close to death from my youth" (Ps 88:15), have always stood out.

The taboo is well-earned. Cold death has no regard for whom it affects. No matter how talented or famous we may be, no matter our fortunes or misfortunes, no matter how strong we grow, we come to an all-too-common end. No exceptions. Death takes no requests and grants no special privileges. Death has no easy version for the beginner, nor an advanced version for the proficient. It never takes a day off. Death has scant variety. It may arrive as the eventual result of natural causes, aging, accident, disease, or violence. History's hardships—war, disease, and famine—escort death across the centuries. Death can always be crueler; its shrill and severe nature stands out all the more when a child dies. Death never compromises nor hears an appeal. We may cry, scream, or pound our fist into the table. Death never reacts. We may reason, repress, or blame. Death doesn't move. Underneath its lethal outer cloak the experience of physical death is the same: It is sharply decisive. The body has *no more* life. Heart and brain function permanently cease. The body turns cold and still. Where does the pain we feel about death come from? It comes from this: there is a *contradiction in existence*. We sense both the paradox of our longing for infinity and the fact that death will swallow us.

Touching the pain: "no more"

As we turned out of the parking lot I fired another question: "What will happen to his body?" My mom gently explained to me in very general and highly nuanced terms what I would later come to know at the process of decay. I responded: "Then why did they put him in a suit?" "Won't that mess up the suit?" My questions were a sign of something. Trepidation at the basic facts I had just observed was sinking in. That touch had proved something for me, and it was rapidly dawning on me: the man lying in that coffin can't do anything, anymore, ever. He can't move. He can't go to work. He can't call anyone on the phone. If he decays, then the *no more* is not only no more. It is a *permanent no more.* He can't go to the beach. He can't hug his kids (and they can't hug him). He can't play baseball. He will have *no more* Christmas mornings, *no more* birthday parties, *no more* time with his family.

The Roman philosopher Cicero was no stranger to the incredible hold the "no more" of death can have on human beings when he commented, "That long while when I shall be no more has more effect on me than this short present time, which nevertheless seems endless to me."[1] Death turns us all into philosophers. That touch at the funeral home made all the abstractions convincingly concrete. And it boiled down to one phrase for me: . . . no more . . . no more. The Book of Job emphasizes the "no more" of death: "But mortals die, and are laid low; humans expire, and where are they? As waters fail from a lake, and a river wastes away and dries up, so mortals lie down and do not rise again; until the heavens are *no more*, they will not awake . . ." (Job 14:10–12). The psalmist agrees and laments

---

1. Cicero, *Letters to Atticus,* VII, 18,1.

that he will "depart and [be] *no more*" (Ps 39:13). The psalmist repeats: "like those forsaken among the dead . . . like those whom you remember *no more*" (Ps 88:5). Other than sacred Scripture, the most important book I have read on death is Nicholas Wolterstorff's *Lament for a Son*. He, too, emphasizes the anguish of the "no more": "The pain of the *no more* outweighs the gratitude of the *once was*."[2]

Over the years I have reflected on the frayed edge of the thread I picked up that afternoon. The thread was the "no more" of death. All I had just walked past that August afternoon had the eerie subdued scream of *no more*. Every *no more* I had ever heard of by the age of ten years old was only temporary: "No more swimming today." "No more going out; it's too dark now." "No more summer vacation once school begins . . . I can't wait until next summer." With those "no mores" the next day always dawned, the pool dependably opened, and summer faithfully returned. Now, however, the *no more* of death seemed fatally final and permanent. I can well understand why many people drop the thread, ignore it, or pretend it does not exist. I can understand why people stop asking questions about death: the questions are simply too heavy. We run from our questions and from the thread. We run from them into alcohol, step over them into drugs, or deny them and plunge headlong into work. We avoid as best we can the reminders of the painful *no more* of death.

The looming inevitable *no more* of death is the reason even the adults were reluctant to go in the funeral home that warm August afternoon, and so quick to depart, even though I had thought they had everything figured out. The *no more* is why my breath hid and my feet stopped as I saw the body in the coffin. *No more*. The line of

---

2. Nicholas Wolterstorff, *Lament for a Son*, 13.

people that had threaded its way from the sidewalk to the porch, then through the hallway and into the viewing room dissipated and disappeared as soon as each one exited the back door into the fresh air. Another thread lurked in that stark house. I had reached out and touched it. I had picked it up and now couldn't let go: the thread of "no more."

The *no more* held my attention. I tugged on it and it pulled me farther. This sense of *no more* was the thread that I wouldn't let go . . . or perhaps it wouldn't let me go. By that, I do not mean I thought about it every day. I went back to playing baseball, lamenting going back to school, and asking to stay out later and later with my friends. I didn't become obsessed or even preoccupied with the experience of the wake. Much less did it drive me to crippling or quivering fear. I forgot about it for periods of time. It did, however, have an initial effect on me. I went on with life, but, over the years, that initial effect has stood out for me. The two memories of that touch and of the crucifix stand out. They formed an unmistakable sequence that became a watershed moment, a life lesson, a bench-mark, and a threshold. Something lingered for me within the *no more*. That was my thread.

CHAPTER THREE

From "No More" to "More Than"

Seeing and touching

As I explored the pain of the *no more*, *something else* began to stir. The crucifix *stood out* for me that day in a way it had *never* done before. My seeing the crucifix that day was *unexpected*. Something credible and compelling took place through my actual ordinary experience. Looking back, with the benefit of many years, I can describe this free movement in my soul as an act of faith. By "act of faith" I do not mean a "guess" or a "leap in the dark." I do not mean a moment of ecstatic euphoria or pristine clarity. Those things may accompany faith, but they are not acts of faith in themselves. I mean quite the opposite. I mean the light of grace shed in the soul by which one recognizes that God is acting.[1] In this light, one is drawn

---

1. See Henri Bouillard, *The Logic of the Faith* (New York: Sheed and Ward, 1967), 1–35; see also, Edith Stein, *The Science of the Cross* (Washington D.C.: ICS Publications, 2002), 72; and Henri De Lubac, *A Brief Catechesis on Nature and Grace* (San Francisco: Ignatius Press, 1984), 80.

to Christ and adheres to him. The movement toward faith is not an escape. It is a free surrender. I had many escape routes available to me in my pain, each more superficial than the next. I could have escaped the pain of death by plunging headlong into getting perfect grades, becoming an extremist of some sort, escaping into the world of drugs, or getting obsessed with video games. But, as he does for every person, God offered me the invitation right there in the middle of my concrete experience and revealed himself in the heart of the act of faith. I could not articulate the intuition or perception in that way at the time. Obscure as the experience was and would remain, reflecting on it nonetheless led me into all that the Church teaches on salvation in Christ.

That day the image of the cross was sealed in my memory, yet I wasn't even thinking about faith or religion that afternoon. Something within the unexpectedness of the truth of the cross of Jesus caught and held on to me. It was not some type of spiritualized painkiller that overtook my emotions of fear. It emerged right in the middle of these very feelings of confusion. Even with the prominence of the cross, I still felt like I was in over my head, somewhere I had never been before. Trying to understand death leaves us stranded in a tangled maze. The more distressed we become, the more confusing the labyrinth-like paths of life close in on us. At these moments our prayer is that of the psalmist: "Make me to know your ways, O LORD; teach me your paths" (Ps 25:4). We wait in faithfulness and patience so that we can one day say, "And thus the paths of those on earth were set right" (Wis 9:18).

After the wake, as I continued questioning, my mother reminded me of the Gospel accounts of Jesus' death and resurrection. She explained that Jesus has conquered death and that, though this man's body was buried in the earth, his soul did not die, but lived on. She continued, pointing out that we hoped his soul lived on in heaven, and that his soul and body would be reunited one day in the general resurrection. I had heard most of these notions at various times in Catholic school or as we prayed the prayers of the Mass. I had general ideas of what they meant. As I kept probing, my questions about the painful thread of *no more* had now led me to faith. My everyday life linked up with Sunday Mass and with my Catholic education in a startling alignment. I can still recall my mother reminding me of the phrase from the Apostles' Creed: "I believe . . . in the resurrection of the body and life everlasting." I firmly believed this then and do so today. Yet, the *no more* of nonexistence and the idea of no return to this life were too big for me to grasp then.

The crucifix on the coffin and my mother's words about the resurrection planted a seed. They invited me—or, more accurately, summoned me—to a living faith. They deepened my vocation. It did not all unfold right away but gradually, over many years. Looking back today, however, I understand how that early discussion was, for me, similar to the words of the psalmist: "The snares of death encompassed me; the pangs of Sheol laid hold on me; I suffered distress and anguish. Then I called on the name of the LORD: 'O LORD, I pray, save my life!' " (Ps 116:3–4) I was moving along the thread, following the clues from *no more* to a distant stirring of *more than*. It felt as if someone had begun to tug ever so slightly on the thread, leading me slowly forward over the years. My experience is not unique. In times of confusion God does not hand us ready-made answers and formulaic solutions. Love is not ready-made or a formula. God is a hidden God. He hides signs of his love all around us, especially in times of hardship and bewilderment. What is hidden, once found, grows strong in our hearts.

God hid something deep in my overriding sensory memories. I could have overlooked those moments or missed them, as I am sure I have missed moments throughout my life in which God was trying to get through to me. That interior *seeing* and *touching* are part of the constellation of actions at the center of the genuine life of faith.

Common objections

Some people may scoff and say I was simply a scared kid who grabbed on to faith in a very painful moment. Some may say that faith was my mother's escape and became mine as well. In short, critics will say I had a hard time dealing with the stark oblivion of death or the doom of nonexistence, so I ran away into the empty consolation of faith. Some may even claim that faith is merely an illusory ceremonial coping mechanism, a naive wish left over from the Middle Ages that the modern world has all but outgrown and dismissed. Yet such a skeptical analysis is hopelessly superficial. Faith always holds *more*. I was reaching out not only to faith, but *also to reason*.

Medical science had determined that the man in the coffin had physically died. His heart had permanently stopped beating and his brain activity had definitively stopped. Physical science had done its job and proved he was indisputably dead. The danger is that a narrow brand of science reduces the mystery of death simply to verifying the physical signs of its presence—the complete and irreversible termination of heart and brain activity. But natural reason is more than biology and physical science. Classical reason relies on more than observation and measurement. Reason also has to do with the remarkable innate capacity we humans have to proceed systematically and clearly from basic principles and reach sound conclusions through logical acts of the mind. While reason does not contradict physical science, it does go greatly beyond the merely observable and measurable domain of science. Reason reads *within* reality. In fact, the very word "intellect" means to "read within," to proceed deeper. Our intellectual reason can go to profound places, which the most powerful microscope or telescope simply cannot reach. Following our reason is not the same thing as being academically "smart" or getting straight A's in class. Reason leads to questions that move beyond what can be observed and measured, and thus reason leads us to faith. The thread leads us farther. But, of course, temptations remain. We must be careful.

The temptation to drop the thread and turn back

We must follow the thread through some dangerous temptations. When we encounter the painful tragedy of the death of those we love, the overarching temptation is to let go of the thread and wander off. The underlying suggestion is that we as individuals know best. The chief temptation then becomes an attempt to find our own way through the puzzling maze. At first, I thought faith meant that God, who is all-powerful and all-loving, should have intervened to miraculously heal this particular man and prevent his death. After my classmate's father died, I asked why God didn't step in with an amazing display of absolute power and raise him from the dead. I wasn't angry at God. As a matter of fact, I was *on God's side*, I thought that such an action would convince everyone that God existed. I thought such a display would bring about faith. Of course, that was a temptation to let go of the thread. The most powerful temptations never appear ugly. They appear to be the best course of action. This is because temptations are illusions. But, remember, illusions thrive on shadows. Illusions need some degree of darkness and confusion in order to survive. In my confusion, I was tempted to reduce the living God to an idol I could control. This is one of the oldest and most common temptations: to reduce faith in the living God to an automatic, flat, and naïve, other-worldly pietism. I wanted God to be immediate and automatic. I would think, "Why didn't God act as *I* thought he should have?"

So often many well-intentioned people today have stopped asking the deeper questions about death, for they no longer see death as a mystery but as an option. On the one hand, we seek solutions to reverse aging and put off death. We invest countless billions of dollars in creating products or seeking genetic discoveries with the hope that they will allow us to stay young. On the other hand, as much as we flee the prospect of death, we *seek death out* and *use* death. People now use death as a *solution* for what is considered inconvenient. In an extreme consumerist lifestyle, we can come to declare a child in the womb an inconvenience or even an enemy. At the same time, a pleasure-driven culture claims that euthanasia is a solution to illness and old age, and a physician should assist with it. Once again, science is used to deliver death. For the modern world, death has also become entertainment, a box office hit. Crowds cheer scenes of death and applaud them on the big screen. It seems as if modern society has, in some ways, fallen in love with death.

Death and atheism

When we lose someone close to us, we are also tempted not only to let go of the thread, but also to run away from it—perhaps even to give up on God or turn against him. It is important to distinguish between the strong feelings of anger that can be generated by grief and an outright atheism. The arguments often proposed by atheists to deny the existence of God frequently have a distinct tenor, sounding more like repeated *complaints* about God. In extreme cases, the complaints maintain that God has not proved his existence to the atheist. The pre-atheist yields to a common temptation: the demand that God intervene not on God's terms, but on *human terms.* When God does not fulfill that demand, the atheist sits in judgment on God and hands down a sentence of non-existence. The atheist stubbornly crosses his arms and demands that God be God on the atheist's terms, not on God's. It seems then that the atheist's god is the self. The atheist wants a manmade God, one that humans can control. The living God does not simply want to convince us once and for all of his almighty power. That is what an *idol* does. Idols are about power, but God is about love (see 1 Jn 4:8, 16; *CCC* 221, 773, and 1604). Pope Francis has pointed out that idols only lead us aimlessly deeper into an immense labyrinth.[2] Because the atheist wants God to be an idol, and God absolutely refuses to be an idol, the atheist rejects God.

It is easy to argue against the existence of idols because, ultimately, idols are empty and worthless. Idols are manmade (see Ps 135:15). Authentic love, on the other hand, is not an argument. It is an unfathomable mystery that yields to deeper love, the love of the living God. The majority of arguments that atheists present are arguments against the existence of a god that atheists say Christians worship: a rule-obsessed, idealistic, distant, and cruel deity who closely watches for any misstep and then delights in severely punishing the offense. I have never met any mature person who believes that such a being exists. But I have met atheists who believe that *Christians believe* in the existence of such a being. Atheists further believe that if they disprove the existence of such a being, then they have disproved the existence of the Christian God. But the being that the atheist denies is not the Christian God and never was. I have never heard an atheist form an effective argument that denies the existence of the *living* God.

---

2. See Pope Francis, *Lumen Fidei* (Boston: Pauline Books & Media, 2013), no. 13.

It may happen that believers or people of good will feel angry at God due to a loss and are then tempted to withdraw from him. It is important to stress that those feelings do not make them atheists. Rather, in their place of loss and pain they are being offered a life-giving thread. On that August afternoon I stood at one of the crossroads of atheism: the temptation to say that God did not exist because he did not live up to the reputation I had attributed to him. He didn't do what I wanted him to do. But faith is not about what I want God to do, or what I insist God do, or what God does not do. Faith is about what he has already done in Christ. Faith is about who God is. This is the thread we hold on to.

CHAPTER FOUR

Holding On

One of the most important facts of living faith is that God's ways are not our ways (see Is 55:8). We often insist on the opposite: that *our* ways be *God's* ways. We are tempted to reverse roles with God. We don't do this with any bad intention. We don't want to overthrow God; we want to help him. We want to tell him our pain and hardship so that he can fix it. Yet, as we do, we tend to repeat the old common mistake: we often want God to use big things as he acts in our lives. So we not only get in our own way, but also in God's way. Our eagerness can slip into stubbornness. Instead of saying, "Speak, Lord, your servant is listening," we often say, "Listen, Lord, your servant is speaking." We want the heavens to part, the lightning bolt to strike and make everything okay. Sometimes we may even be tempted to give up on God because we feel he doesn't deliver as we think he should.

It may seem as if we expect too much from God, but in fact we expect far too little. We take a greater risk when we let go of insisting on our own ways and set out to learn God's ways. In the Gospel, Jesus tells us that his mystery can hide even in something as common as a cup of cold water (see Mt 10:42) or an ordinary seed (see Mt 13:31–32). God is never outdone in his wise and loving plan. When he seems absent, he is closer than ever. God's plan aligns what may seem to be a minor detail or an ordinary event, and fills it with more meaning than we can imagine. Hugh of Balma, the noted thirteenth-century Carthusian, tells us that God makes countless attempts night and day, countless times each hour, to draw us to himself.[1]

It can take a long time to sense and follow the deep curves of God's action. It has taken me almost forty years, but I have begun to trace out and understand the frontiers of the paths that God took when I first encountered the reality of death. This I know: God accompanied every person who entered the funeral home that day, as he has each person who has ever faced death. I certainly don't mean that a private revelation took place or that death was somehow good. But I do mean that even in the midst of death, hardship, and suffering, the Holy Spirit eagerly works to bring forth a precious good in our lives. The Spirit's work points to the deep dimensions of the saving action of Jesus Christ in his ultimate victory over sin and death. God is acting even in times of tremendous grief. Moments of anguish and heartache are invitations to follow the thread into deeper faith. God uses everything to draw us into his mystery. God is a God of love, and true to its deepest nature, love uses hidden ways we otherwise could never predict or expect. With God, what seems incidental, ordinary, or apparent is often filled with untold grace and indescribable meaning. *Love loves to hide in the obvious.*

---

1. See Hugh of Balma, "The Roads to Zion Mourn" in *Carthusian Spirituality: The Writings of Hugh of Balma and Guigo de Ponte.* The Classics of Western Spirituality Series (Mahwah, NJ: Paulist Press, 1997), 71.

The Book of Wisdom tells us: "God did not make death, and he does not delight in the death of the living" (Wis 1:13; see Rom 5:12, James 1:15, and Gn 3). God takes no pleasure in anyone's death (see Ez 18:32). As I look back I can now see that God was acting as I encountered the effects of death that day. In fact, God acted more wondrously than if he had, by an act of sheer autonomous power, reanimated the corpse of the dead man.

The family: God's preference for the obvious

The first and most general movement of God on that afternoon was that my family was *together as a family*. This may seem insignificant, but, at least for me, a deeper truth was at work. I mean that God was acting for me in the very circumstance that I entered *with* my family.

It seems obvious, doesn't it? In my first ten years of life wherever I went, I went mostly with my family. Being part of a family is as ordinary and unremarkable as it gets. Like many families, if we went on vacation, we went together. If we visited relatives for a party or dinner, we did so together. If we went out to eat at a restaurant, we usually went together. Even when I went to school, practice, or a game, my parents and family attended. If we did spend a night apart for one reason or another, we soon came back to that natural bond of unconditional love.

Sadly, due to human frailty and our fallen human nature, we may carry unhealed wounds, old grudges, and unresolved hurts from our family. Some people have been used or betrayed by family members. Still others have been upset, offended, or distressed. Even in the midst of difficulty, dysfunction, and pain, the family is *meant* to be the place of unconditional love. That may be why family-pain is among the most difficult to bear. "Unconditional love" doesn't mean a picture-perfect or storybook ideal. Even in family situations where signs of love are scarce, love will not permanently desert us. Love finds a way. Love is *somewhere*, perhaps in those who drew us forth from the pain. God uses many people and instruments to show the path of love. No pain is beyond the reach of God's grace and mercy. God can heal even events long past and transform the past anew. His healing points to love. And however faint or obscure it may seem, authentic love always points to the eternal. It points to living faith, which is about a real relationship with a *Person*, Jesus Christ, the Son of God, in and through his Church.

I was overwhelmed when I brushed up against my own finitude for the very first time. I began to feel that the thread is not just loosely tied to some distant fixture, but it may be moored to a firm buttress. And here is where the deep action of God was so close and unexpected that it seemed far away: The first time I met the stark unmistakable coldness of death I did so in the familiar warmth of my family.

We were not the model family, nor were we flawless—far from it. But we walked in as a family, wounds and all. And that meant something to me. My family did not shield me from the signs of death. My parents decided that even at my young age I could walk into that funeral home room. They knew it would be the first time I would see a dead person. My parents allowed me to experience something that would awaken me to the transcendent. Perhaps they were not even completely aware of that, and they may even have decided I should go simply on the basis of good manners and propriety. But something else happened. Something or Someone *more* unfolded and stepped into play, stepped—we might say—into the maze.

It may seem that I am making a lot out of a small circumstance, a mundane, routine fact. But, I believe it is more. I believe this is a clue. Small things hold mysteries much larger than themselves. Anaxagoras, the Greek philosopher, said, "There is no limit to what is small, for there is always something smaller."[2] Smallness contains unlimited mysteries. Pope Benedict XVI pointed out that "the origins of anything new have always been small, practically invisible, and easily overlooked. . . . The great—the mighty—is ultimately the small. . . . Is it not what seems so small that is truly great?"[3] Clues hide in otherwise small, routine moments. That is why clues are easily overlooked and often missed. On its narrow surface, it was an occasion to pay condolences and express sympathies. Seen in its transcendent depths, it was a confrontation that takes a lifetime to grasp. Finitude and infinity pointed to each other in a movement that escaped ordinary focus. In the interplay of that moment something opened up, raged in the stillness, and I glimpsed a light that radiated forth. An otherwise incidental courtesy cloaked depths it could never know.

God allowed something quite *definitive* to happen as my family and I stopped cold in front of that coffin. We were in the presence of far *more than* we knew. Eternity hides, not in fanfare or lightning bolts, but inside still, small moments, crouching only inches beneath the obvious. We can easily miss what is right in front of our eyes every day. As my father's hand moved me along and I stared wide-eyed and open-mouthed, overwhelmed at human finitude, I did so simultaneously from the unconditional love and protection of my family. In that moment human finitude intersected, crisscrossed, and collided with the infinite. I stood at the crossroads of time and eternity. God opened up and permitted me to glimpse and even to

---

2. Anaxagoras, from *Fragment 3*, as in Paolo Zellini, "A Brief History of Infinity," trans. David Marsh (New York: Penguin Books, 2005), 8.

3. Pope Benedict XVI, *Jesus of Nazareth part II, Holy Week: From the Entrance into Jerusalem to the Resurrection* (Vatican City: *Libreria Editrice Vaticana*, 2011), 247. On the importance of smallness and its ability to convey significance, see Donna Tartt, *The Goldfinch*, 24.

be drawn into the intense and anguished "no more" of human finitude as it clashed with the unmistakable everyday signs of his absolute and infinite love. The line of people going into the funeral home approached the limited, human side of the threshold of the finite and the infinite.

Others may have entered the funeral home that day without their family, or upset with or separated from their family. But God extends threads to each person on their journey. Remember, God's ways are not our ways. God prefers the hidden, and he hides in the obvious. Even the ordinary and mundane cannot escape God's radiance. The light of Christ *underlies* all of history and existence. His light is so bright that we mistake it for darkness. His ways can seem like folly to us. The light does not *explain* the mystery; it guides us *into the mystery* and makes a living claim on us. Most importantly, light reveals truth—and truth battles back the shadowy darkness of confusion in which temptation thrives.

The upheaval of death takes time to sort through. It is excruciatingly difficult to step onto sacred ground and into the unbearable light where life meets death and death meets life eternal. Everything in our daily life, indeed everything in history, converges on Jesus Christ and radiates forth from him in such a way that the brilliant light of Christ fills all things with a fullness that is unbearable.[4]

---

4. See Hans Urs von Balthasar, *Theodrama Theological Dramatic Theory II: Dramatis Personae: Man in God* (San Francisco: Ignatius Press, 1990), 63.

CHAPTER FIVE

The First Clue: Existence

Death has few rules. One is that death has to take place some-where. It does not occur in a vacuum. Most generally, death occurs *within existence*. Only things that have life and exist can die. This may seem blatantly obvious, yet the obvious is important. In our hurt, fear, and distress over the death of a loved one, we often demand immediate answers. I certainly did. If we rush to seek an immediate answer, we can easily hurry past the obvious and the abundant clues it provides. Usually, finding answers begins with patience. Just as life has no shortcuts or quick fixes, neither does the mystery of death. Any apparent shortcut is really a trap disguised to look like the easy way out.

My first impulse was to explain death, to find an answer. Following our impulses can get us hopelessly lost in the twisting cor-ners of the maze. Over the years I have returned to patience as the thread that first led me backward, to earlier experiences in my life, to help bring me understanding. If I had followed my instincts I would have rushed forward to force my way out of the perplexing maze. The thread led me in another direction—to places I had already been in order to pick up truths I had not seen so clearly. I have been grateful for that detour.

An investigation, tracing the thread, begins at the beginning, not the middle. It traces the thread back to the beginning to look for more clues along the way. If we want to learn about the final moment of our individual, human, earthly existence, we must turn first to our beginnings. One of my earliest clues was that the mystery of death takes place within a wider mystery, the mystery of human existence. So the first question about the mystery of death is: What is existence in general and, more specifically, what is human existence?

Gardens: perennial truths

Sacred Scripture is a classic source of understanding human origins. The Bible tells us that human existence began in a garden: "And the LORD God planted a garden in Eden, in the east; and there he put the man whom he had formed" (Gn 2:8). God entrusted the garden to man, "to till it and keep it" (Gn 2:15). Man was to "have dominion" over creation (Gn 1:26; 28). This garden was also the place in which human beings discovered what it means *to exist*. Man was placed on the earth for a task: to cultivate the soil (see Gn 2:15), to name the animals (see Gn 2:19), and to have dominion over the earth (see Gn 1:28). In the Garden, man discovered important truths about the nature of existence.

It's a long way from the Garden of Eden, but my parents planted a large vegetable garden in our backyard each spring. Gardens are patient places. They have time-tested truths to teach us about human existence. The first step in learning about God is to repeatedly "circle around" things that exist. When we look closely, from every angle, at what is, sooner or later we are drawn into amazement at the fundamental mystery of the transcendence that underlies the inmost reality of all that is. This is the fundamental task of a child. Balthasar points out that even though the creation of the world is God's most serious responsibility, the wisdom at God's side treats the whole endeavor as a form of play: "When he marked out the foundations of the earth, then I was beside him, like a master worker; and I was daily his delight, rejoicing before him always, rejoicing in his inhabited world and delighting in the human race" (Prov 8:29–31).[1]

A child's ingenious play penetrates the simple profundity of creation. Jesus rejoices in this very truth: "I give praise to you, Father, Lord of heaven and earth, for although you have hidden these things from the wise and the learned you have revealed them to the childlike" (Mt 11:25 NAB). If we patiently trace and follow it, existence has a depth that recedes into mystery. A child has an original brilliance by which his or her imagination naturally seeks out the multiple hidden mysteries behind everyday, obvious, seemingly mundane realities. There is no better place to "circle around" reality than a garden. I was in a garden before I could walk. And I learned a lot there about existence.

Rocks

As a young child I was captivated by the existence of rocks. The town where I grew up, Roxborough, had earned its name; countless rocks of all sizes lay just beneath the soil throughout our backyard. I could stand for hours and throw rocks into the river near our house. I learned that because rocks are so hard and impenetrable, they can

---

1. Hans Urs von Balthasar, *Explorations in Theology V: Man Is Created* (San Francisco: Ignatius Press, 2014), 216.

withstand severe weather, making them well suited for shelter and safety. It is the nature of a rock to have mass, volume, and weight. Another obvious truth I learned early in the garden is that you can't use a seed or a plant the same way you can use a rock. Behind all of these elementary observations was a deeper truth that many of us take for granted: within existence there is tremendous variety. Things are not all the same; different things have their own natures and abide by various laws. I also learned a deeper truth: We don't create those basic natural laws. We *discover* them already in existence.

Tomatoes

As the clues about rocks were piling up, I learned more about the garden. God gave "every plant yielding seed" and "every tree with seed in its fruit" to us for food (Gn 1:29). Centuries of interaction with soil, seed, and rocks taught us a lot about the mystery of plants, fruit, and vegetables—tomatoes, for example. It may seem like a wide detour to discuss rocks and tomatoes in a book about death and eternal life, but ancient wisdom and everyday common sense both tell us that the mysteries of life are not neatly divided into separate packages. The mysteries of life are all connected.

As I spent time in the garden I discovered that seeds hold a lot of mystery. I was amazed that the small seed we dropped in the ground in early April would become, in a matter of weeks, a large plant. How had it happened? I had watched a seed become a small shoot, then a leaf, then a stem under the leaf. But none of that could have fit in the seed. So where did it all come from? Jesus compares this daily mystery to the Kingdom of God (see Mk 4:27).

Over the centuries human beings have learned the mystery of how plants and vegetables grow. This mystery is not magic. It is far more: the unchangeable truth about the nature and meaning of mineral existence and vegetative life, as well as warmth, sunlight, water, and soil.

Rex

Besides a vegetable garden, we also had a dog named Rex. It was obvious to me that, like minerals and vegetable life, Rex existed. He would come running up to me and knock me down. Animals have things in common with minerals and with vegetative life, but, unlike the minerals and like the vegetables, Rex was alive. Rocks aren't alive. Plants and animals are. Plants and animals can take in nourishment, grow, and reproduce. Of course, plants and animals do these things in far different ways. Yet, I knew Rex could do things no tomato plant ever could.

Whenever we were in the yard and thunder clouds rolled in, Rex ran around the yard barking. He would zoom toward the door to go into the house and down the cellar. Animal life has something that far outstrips vegetative life. Animals have the instinct to seek shelter.

Rex liked to do something, in season and out, that no plant could do. He liked to dig. Rex would dig up the garden soil to bury a bone. It was part of his nature. I also liked to dig. But, unlike Rex, all my parents had to do to stop me was teach me not to dig in the garden. They showed me what it would do to the seeds and the plants. I learned and understood that the garden was for food, not for games. So I took my shovel and went off to another part of the yard where it was okay to dig. Rex could not be taught. He could be trained, but even with the best of training, he simply could not resist the instinct to dig in the garden.

Instinct is an unlearned behavior necessary for survival. Survival instincts are strong. Rex dug in the garden because he had inherited this instinct from his wild nature. It could not be tamed out of him because this survival instinct to preserve food was so deeply rooted. I had learned more of those basic truths about instinct and existence: out of instinct, Rex would seek food and shelter; he would dig, race around, and bark.

The momentum in existence

So where do all of the obvious truths about existence lead us? They lead us through existence to a deeper and more astounding truth. Things made of mere matter, such as rocks, need to be moved by something outside themselves; vegetative life can move from within; animals move from within in an instinctual sense; but only humans move themselves in a rational sense.[2] The very basic yet time-tested truths about agriculture, animal life, and human life tell us something not only about farming, wildlife, and society, but about existence itself. Something is going on in nature and in existence. Human beings have the capacity to discover an intelligible *momentum* in existence itself. Whether it is a rock, a tomato, a dog, or another human being, our questions unlock the clues hidden in experience. We learn the truths of the nature of created things. The things I learned in the garden were true not simply in the early 1970s—they had always been true. The ancient insights found in the Book of Wisdom express the very same truths:

> For it is he who gave me unerring knowledge of what exists, to know the structure of the world and the activity of the elements; the beginning and end and middle of times, the alternations of the solstices and the changes of the seasons, the cycles of the year and the constellations of the stars, the natures of animals and the tempers of wild animals, the powers of spirits and the thoughts of human beings, the varieties of plants

---

2. See Saint Thomas Aquinas, *Summa Theologiae* I., q. 93 a 2. See also the Tree of Porphyry in *Porphyry the Phoenician* "Isagoge", translation, introduction, and notes by E. W. Warren (The Pontifical Institute of Mediaeval Studies), 35–47. See also Hans Urs von Balthasar, *Theodrama II*, 218 and 249; *The Glory of the Lord I*, 21, 391, *The Glory of the Lord II*, 107.

and the virtues of roots; I learned both what is secret and what
is manifest, for wisdom, the fashioner of all things, taught me.
(Wis 7:17–22)

Further, the truths I learned in the garden were true all around
the world. The common and practical daily experience of human
beings reveals reasonable and ageless truths, precious clues to the
deep mystery of existence, of our humanity, of life and of death.
These clues, as any good clue does, lead to the mysterious nature of
humanity.

Created in the image and likeness of God

As I ran around our yard near the garden I learned that something incredible was going on—not only deep in the soil, deep in
the tomato, or deep in Rex, but also *deep inside of me*—things we
often take for granted. When we step back and consider the mystery
of humanity, a profound arc begins to take shape. We realize that
human beings are not simply a higher level of animal. Human beings
participate in the order of creation in a completely different way
than animals, plants, and minerals. As I discovered and learned the
truths of existence, I was exercising a capacity only humans can exercise. I didn't just learn what was going on in the laws of nature. I
learned that I learned what was going on. I didn't simply know what
was going on; I knew that I knew what was going on.

Human beings have the capacity to know and to understand the
nature of things. Think about that for a moment. Rex did not know
he was a dog. Rex could hear sounds; he could hear everything that
I heard. But Rex heard noises; I can hear Mozart. Rex could see
lights and shadows, but I can see a Monet. An animal acts out of
instinct, but no animal can understand, much less explain, instinct.
Humans can.

In my childhood, the garden taught me the enduring treasured truth of the order of existence and human nature. I discovered I, as a human being, had the capacity for consciousness, self-awareness, and self-determination in a way unlike any other being in the visible universe. Human beings have the capacity to know and understand the order of reality, and to choose to love freely the good that exists within that order. We discover, deep in our being, our capacity for conscience. As we discover the human capacity for intellect and will, something essential and self-evident is triggered in our interior depth. The word "capacity" is important. It is the very notion that the *Catechism of the Catholic Church* uses to describe man's depth in the order of grace (see *CCC* 357, 1704). The capacity to know and to love reveals something about human beings. The capacity to know and to love means you and I have the ability to participate in existence in an unprecedented way. Animals participate in existence by instinct. Humans can do so by knowing the truth with our intellect and by loving the good with our will. Our reason clearly tells us that we are different from all of creation. And our difference sets us apart and places utterly unique responsibilities and duties upon us. Before we ever have the ability to solve a mathematical equation, to form a sentence, or to learn about a garden, as a human being we have the innate capacity to do so. The embryo, the child in the womb, the terminally ill, the person in a vegetative state all have the innate capacity to know and to love.

This is why the Book of Genesis tells us that God created human beings in his own image and likeness: "Then God said: 'Let us make human beings in our image, after our likeness. Let them have dominion over the fish of the sea, the birds of the air, the tame animals, all the wild animals, and all the creatures that crawl on the earth. God created mankind in his image; in the image of God he created them; male and female he created them'" (Gn 1:26–27 NABRE; see Wis 2:23, Sir 17:3, and Jas 3:9). From the very first moment of his existence, man is in a relationship with God that far outstrips the rest of the visible world. Man is the image of God according to his intellectual nature and reason.[3] The Second Vatican Council affirms this fundamental truth, "For sacred Scripture teaches that humankind was created 'in the image of God,' with the capacity to know and love its creator, and was divinely appointed with authority over all earthly creatures, to rule and use them and glorify God."[4]

Since we are made in the image of God, we are also *capax Dei*, a Latin phrase meaning *capable of God*. It means that we have the *capacity for God*; from the moment of conception each human being is destined to be in relationship with God, to know and love God. Of all the creatures in the visible world, "[man] alone is called to share, by knowledge and love, in God's own life" (*CCC* 356). This is why human life has inviolable dignity from the first moment of conception and must be treated with the utmost respect to natural death. We must treat the human being, born or unborn, incurably sick or healthy, as one who bears the breath of God within.

The human soul

Our capacity for intellect and will cannot be traced back simply to something physical in the order of nature. Our intellect and will are not, at their root, biological or merely psychological. Our intellect and will testify to their being rooted in and revealing our profound spiritual nature and the order of grace. Our capacity to

---

3. *Summa Theologiae* Ia q3 a1 ad 2; q 93 a6 *sed contra*, a6 ad 2, a7.
4. Second Vatican Council, *Gaudium et Spes,* (Boston: Pauline Books & Media, 1965), no. 12. See Luis Ladaria, SJ, "Humanity in the Light of Christ in the Second Vatican Council" *Vatican II: Assessment and Perspectives, Volume II,* Rene Latourelle, SJ, ed. (New Jersey: Paulist Press, 1989), 388.

know with our intellect and to love with our will points directly to the existence of the transcendent principle of life at work in us that goes beyond the physical, corporeal, or biological. This principle of life is our invisible, spiritual, and immortal soul (*CCC* 33, 1703, 1705).

The soul is an incorporeal living substance that truly underlies our existence and subsists in us. As Saint Augustine and Saint Thomas taught, man is not merely a soul or a body, but the union of soul and body such that the soul is the form of the body.[5] The soul is not created by the parents of the child, nor does it pre-exist the person. The human soul is created immediately by God (see Gn 2:7). The *Catechism* tells us that the soul is the spiritual principle of the human being. The soul is not like the body's motor, nor does it reside simply in the mind. It is the deepest dimension of man's being. The soul is the very form of the body such that the whole soul is in every part of the body at once.[6] Our intelligence and will are rooted in the soul alone and remain in the soul after death.[7] As such, the human soul in each human being is individual and immortal; it does not die when it separates from the body at the moment of personal death. The soul is reunited with the body at the resurrection of the dead. This does not make the body second class, however. Saint Pope John Paul II taught that the human person becomes aware of his esteemed calling in and through his body. The human body, as well as the person's spiritual nature, is vital to the dignity of his being created in the image of God. The Second Vatican Council teaches:

---

5. See Saint Augustine, *De Civitate Dei*, 19.3; see also Saint Thomas Aquinas, *Summa Theologiae* I, q. 75, art., 4 *sec contra*; q. 76, art., 1. See also *CCC* 362, 365; and Auer, Ratzinger, *Eschatology: Death and Eternal Life*, 148–149; *DS* 902, 1440.

6. See *Summa Theologiae*, I, q. 76, art., 8 and q. 93, art., 2.

7. See Ibid., I, q. 77, art., 8.

"Though made of body and soul, man is one. Through his bodily composition he gathers to himself the elements of the material world; thus they reach their crown through him."[8]

In our capacity to know and to love we are aware that our own nature, human nature, transcends that of material existence, vegetative existence, and animal existence. With our intellect we search for meaning, and with our will we can love the purpose we find within our existence. This search can only be fulfilled in the order of grace. To say that we are made in the image and likeness of God does not mean that we are God's equals. Saint Thomas tells us that human beings come nearer to God, as his image, than all other things in the visible world because humans have the capacity to know and understand. This nearness means that, by God's generous decision, we are like God and can imitate him in a unique way. But, we are *not* God. Every effect is like its cause, but no effect is greater than its cause. Our likeness to God also means that, in our freedom, we depend upon God. This dependency is not a bad thing or an addiction. The intersection of the infinite and the contingent is not a contradiction, but an *opening*. In this strong reliance upon God, we find the ultimate purpose and meaning of our existence. We continually find a restless yearning at the deep center of our existence. We set out in search from this center. The yearning never wears out; it never gives up. Our yearning cannot be reduced to an overly ambitious attitude, agitated hankering, or fidgety craving. The persistent restless yearning is hard-wired into the *meaning* of life and of human existence. Our yearning leads to the second clue that we discover at reason's edge.

---

8. *Gaudium et Spes,* no. 14.

CHAPTER SIX

The Second Clue: At Reason's Edge

Consider our path thus far. I wouldn't let go of my questions about death, which rose up naturally as I attended my first wake service. Those questions led me to the beginning, to examine the nature of existence. Being and reality hold deep mysteries. As I learned the nature of the various forms of existence, I saw in bold relief what many take for granted: that there is a momentum in existence. The human being, created body and soul in the image and likeness of God, experiences a profound depth. The human soul and, in particular, our vast yearning opens us to untold vistas on the nature of human existence. The human soul knocks on the door of the mystery of immortality.

We know from day-to-day experience that the human spirit cannot be contained. Our enduring yearning has innumerable outlets. We search out the grandest and most exotic adventures. The farthest reaches of the universe cannot satisfy us. We aim the most powerful telescopes at the farthest reaches of the farthest galaxy. We can point high-density microscopes at the tiniest cell in the human body. We can probe the mysteries of the human brain and ponder the laws of subatomic matter. Every generation brings new human energy by which we make groundbreaking discoveries and inventions. Our vitality propels us to cross new frontiers and reach for distant horizons. We devise exciting means of recreation, sports, and literature. We detect the fundamental drive of our infinite yearning strongly at work even in the most routine moments of our daily life. We never tire of relationships by which we seek renewal and fulfillment. Yet, no matter how grand or consequential, every visible thing we have ever found on our own initiative is finite. If we depart from what is integral to our nature as we explore our deep yearning, we brush up against catastrophic dangers. While we experience an infinite longing, we ourselves are finite. If at any time we mistakenly think our inner infinite yearning means that we ourselves are infinite, reality is at hand to teach us yet again that we are finite. But we are slow to learn.

From the garden to the toy store

A story can help to illustrate this point. Just as I was learning the mysteries of the garden, I stumbled upon a place that held a similar allurement: the marketplace. Before I was old enough to go to school I would spend every day with my mother. Several days a week we would go food shopping at the local supermarket, and then stop at a nearby deli for lunch meat. On the way to the deli we had to walk past a toy store. It wasn't just any toy store. It was a huge toy store with floor-to-ceiling windows. Every new wind-'em-up, glitzy gadget and hottest game was on colorful display on the other side of that window—just beyond my reach. Every time we went from the supermarket to the deli we had to walk past those windows the whole length of the toy store. Without fail, as the toy store windows came into view, my eyes doubled in size. While we walked past I began the familiar dance of trying to twist my hand free of my mother's hand. I'd be pointing and pleading, negotiating and begging, promising the best behavior and making the grandest deals; "If I get that race car I will never want another thing. Ever. I mean it." Often my mom would literally drag me past the windows. I'd cry, demand, and dig in my feet.

Toy stores are never far away. We may grow up, but we never outgrow the yearning. The toys change, but the intensity of our search does not. We humans see a lot of things that we want. We reach and grasp for things that we think will make us happy. However, even if they satisfy us for a while, things never completely fulfill us. Satisfaction and fulfillment are not the same thing. When I was four years old I wanted a toy race car. At six I wanted a bicycle. At ten I wanted a racing bike. At sixteen I wanted a car. The sense of yearning remained the same, but the object of the yearning did not. We move from wanting the grades, the fashions, and the popularity. We search after the promotion, the pleasure, and the payoff. The luster of this or that toy may wear off, but the deeper yearning never wears off. Getting everything we want is not the answer. It is the enemy. If getting what we wanted were the answer, then all rich people would be very happy. But we know that many very rich people are very unhappy. Headlines remind us daily that the best things in life aren't things.

Our yearning as a clue

Our yearning is another *clue*. All the "things" we want point to something. That race car and everything else I wanted were signs of something deeper. Our wanting things is not about the things, it is about our wanting. Humans yearn for more. When we "get" what we think will make us happy, it only satisfies us for a while. It does not fulfill us. The natural beauty of a sunset, of an ocean wave, and of a spectacular mountain range deepens our hunger for beauty. A healthy friendship leaves us looking forward to the next conversation. An enthralling novel draws us to turn the next page. A competitive baseball game pulls us to the next inning. A magnificent symphony lures us to the next note. Most beautifully, a husband and wife, after years of happy marriage, are drawn wordlessly and more deeply to surrender freely, yet again, to one another. Their innumerable sacrifices and secrets of love—built, suffered, and shared over a lifetime of days, known mostly only to one another—are daily invitations to even deeper love. Our ceaseless stamina for good hobbies, nourishing pastimes, and wholesome interests reveals something about a boundless desire within us. God made a beautiful world and has given human beings gifts of craftsmanship and ingenuity. No matter what we discover or invent, another realm remains, one that eludes and nonetheless fascinates us. We cannot fully manipulate or completely control this realm, but it draws us forward. Our deep yearning is never exhausted.

Joy and grief are not only profound human emotions, but they are also clues. The news that a mother has conceived new life in her womb brings a most original vintage of sheer joy. Even though we can explain the familiar science of conception, the joy tells us that conception is a miracle. We mistakenly believe that miracles, simply because they are miracles, cannot be common. The miracle of the conception of human life has taken place literally billions of times throughout history. Yet, the specific new human life that is conceived is always utterly distinctive and unique. So is the joy that ought to accompany it. The mixture of the familiar and the surprising coalesces to overflow with overwhelming joy. The joy tells us something about the miracle and the mystery that has taken place. The joy is our surprise at life itself. The emotion confirms our bewilderment at an unmistakable newness that far surpasses our wildest expectations. Joy is a natural clue that God hides in the perfectly ordinary events of life.

Could it be that, like joy, grief is also a natural clue? It is a commonly known fact that every living human being will one day die. The science is clear. Yet, the specific death of the individual person we love brings a most rare and original burden of sorrow and heartache. Could it be that the grief tells us something about the mystery (and the miracle) that has taken place? When those whom we love die, it is important to feel the grief and the pain of that loss. Grief feels like a lead weight that sits immovably in the pit of our stomach as a monument to the fact that life as we knew it is now changed forever. The heartache of mourning feels strange and disturbing. It may descend all at once or come in waves as an ocean tide. We see the things that belonged to our loved one: his or her sweater, car keys, eyeglasses, or favorite chair. When we come upon such familiar objects for the first time after our loved one's passing, these small reminders disorient us. Once they pointed to our loved one's presence. But now they trigger a startling, unexpected emptiness. We feel the presence of an absence. The entire year after the loss is a series of "firsts." We have the first Christmas without them the first birthday, the first wedding, etc. We wish they could step out of photographs and be with us once again. We come across letters or notes they had written at one time or another. Then the first anniversary of their death approaches. Their death changes our experience of time itself. We now begin to measure how long we have lived without them. And all the while, grief weighs us down. The memories and the grief witness to something.

Our grief is evidence of our yearning. And the clue is this: surrounded by endless evidence of our finitude, we yearn for a fulfillment that is infinite. Ultimately, human fulfillment always brings us the deeper knowledge that we are dependent on Another. We are dependent, ultimately, upon God. This Other, God, who is independent, nonetheless freely desires to be in a continuous relationship with us and to develop a history with us. This is the great drama behind everything that is: God, who needs nothing else, longs to share his life with us. "God, infinitely perfect and blessed in himself, in a plan of sheer goodness freely created man to make him share in his own blessed life" (*CCC* 1). Our yearning for the infinite breaks through in the thousand legitimate yearnings we experience every day. My yearning for the toys was a clue. Our yearning for this or that individual thing is a hint, a reminder, a trace of a much deeper yearning. You and I have an infinite yearning deep within us. This infinite yearning, self-evident to each of us, was my next clue.

The contingent yearning for the Infinite

The silence I experienced and the questions at the funeral home so long ago came from the same place. Everyone in line that afternoon glimpsed their finitude. Everyone in the line caught sight of the immense human contradiction: the irrefutable fact that human beings yearn for the infinite while we sense the horrible lurking omen of our own definitive finitude.[1]

Indeed, death runs squarely against the innate awareness within each of us that we are meant for more. Death flies in the face of existence itself. We rebel against death not simply because we are afraid of it, but because we have the deep and abiding sense, going well beyond a hunch or simple instinct, that we were meant for more than death. Human existence itself tells us something by its very longing and desire. Human beings universally attest to a breakthrough from the very depth of their being. We yearn for the infinite. This deep-rooted sense of forever, this yearning for the infinite comes from somewhere—or we could not imagine it. Every effect

---

1. See Henri J. M. Nouwen, *A Letter of Consolation* (New York: HarperCollins Publishers, 1982), 28.

has a cause. As Plato said, "The eye seeks light because it contains something light-like."2 What, then, is the cause of the spiritual capacity of the soul and the infinite yearning we experience? The cry is not from the world. It is a cry for more than the world. The infinite yearning we experience in the order of nature can only be caused by an infinite cause in the order of grace. Our reaction to death cannot arise simply from instinct, sentimentality, or wistful nostalgia for bygone days. Our longing is far more than a melancholy throb. *The innate grief and deep rebellion that human beings experience in the face of death is a reflection of this yearning for the infinite.* We were meant to live forever, and this meaning stands out in bold relief as we face death. And therefore, questions emerge.

We have now arrived at a very important threshold. We can explore this infinite longing with our reason. Natural reason testifies that we find a space within us that calls out for the infinite. It is similar to standing before the seed and sensing the plant and the fruit, even though one can see neither. Instinct does not tell us that fruit comes from the seed; reason does. The *Catechism of the Catholic Church* affirms, "The desire for God is written in the human heart, because man is created by God and for God; and God never ceases to call man to himself" (*CCC* 27). The yearning for the absolute is so unmistakable because it emerges from the very heart of man and is the source of the search for meaning. It is within man, yet transcends man. Saint Augustine said, "For you have made us for yourself, [O Lord], and our heart is restless until it rests in you."3

This truth is so self-evident that we can fail to recognize it. One of the great tasks of the New Evangelization is to restore to us in an

---

2. Plato, *Timaeus*, 45b–d.

3. Saint Augustine, *Confessions* 1.1.1. The author is grateful to Reverend Monsignor Ronny E. Jenkins for this translation.

explicit manner the undeniable awareness of our grand calling and dignity. Death seems so alien to us precisely because something of *forever* lies within us. We can sense it. We can imagine forever. Because human beings have a beginning, the moment of our conception, we cannot imagine what it is to have always existed, to have no beginning. Only God is *eternal*, that is, without beginning *or* end. We can, however, imagine *forever*, immortality. As I gazed into the coffin at the wake I was not simply sensing the fear of the nothingness of death, anxiety at its spookiness, or panic that those around me would also one day die. I was, in fact, sensing the *more than*. I had stumbled upon that beautiful notion of the Book of Ecclesiastes: "God . . . has put the timeless into their hearts so they cannot find out, from beginning to end, the work which God has done" (3:11 NABRE). I was sensing the transcendence of the human person. I was discovering that *death doesn't fit*. In the light of all the meaning, purpose, and beauty of the world around me, death simply didn't fit. It didn't fit with goodness. Death had won the battle in a man's physical life, but not the war.

The deep places of Being

In both our external and our internal world we learn the nature of existence; we discover a momentum at the heart of all that is. And the thread we have been following will lead us along this tremendous momentum to untold mystery. From the immense cosmos to the most miniscule subatomic particle, we detect a distinct energy, purpose, and design at work underneath and deep within all things.

The next question that emerges is: What keeps things in existence? What maintains the material world? What maintains and upholds our internal world? Reason invites us to ask questions that penetrate into the energy beneath existence, beyond what we can see, hear, and touch, toward its deepest, well-reasoned foundation.

As we survey existence we begin to hone in on the *more than*, on the nature of things, and the nature of existence itself. As we accept reason's gracious invitation, we begin to discover the inner brilliance that lies there.

We gaze with inspiration at the bewildering array of endless vitality that continually develops all around us. The human mind continually discerns congruence, intelligibility, and order around every corner of the vast cosmos. We marvel at the complex motion of the planets, the timing of the tides, and the intricacy of the human body. The genius of the psalmist captures the wonder: "The world will surely stand in place, never to be moved. Your throne stands firm from of old; you are from everlasting . . . more powerful than the breakers of the sea powerful in the heavens is the LORD" (Ps 93:1–2, 4 NABRE). The order of nature in the visible world calls us beyond itself to the order of grace.

The laws of existence in the order of nature have much to tell us. For example, the earth on which we live is tilted at an angle of twenty-three and a half degrees. That sounds like a random and arbitrary fact. But consider this: If the angle of the earth were only one degree different, there would be no seasons.[4] Without seasons there would be no gardens, and without them there would be no life. Those 23.5 degrees are crucial to the development of life and of human existence. Consider this as well: The air we need to breathe contains the exact levels of oxygen necessary to sustain human life. At the same time, the crust of the earth is thirty miles wide at its thickest point. If that crust were only ten feet thicker, there would be no oxygen and, therefore, no human life. The thread we follow

---

4. Thomas Dubay, S.M., *The Evidential Power of Beauty: Science and Theology Meet* (San Francisco: Ignatius Press, 1999), 215.

through existence repeatedly reveals to us that the most precise details of nature matter. If these details admitted of the smallest variation, human life would not have developed.[5] Nature brims with intelligible order.

When we encounter tragedy we know its pain so well because tragedy conflicts with the natural order. The staggering beauty of the order of nature, with all of its inexhaustible fertility and harmony, leads us to ask about the origin of the world. Natural reason causes us to sense that existence is no accident. The pattern and purpose that fill the world do not arise as the by-product of blind chance. Complex design does not randomly cause itself or spontaneously generate from a primeval soup.

The created order in the visible universe simply cannot regress to an anonymous infinity. Rather, such order points us in another direction. Where there is design there must be a designer. We can discover clues that the reason behind the world's total reality can only be an absolute and infinite being. The observable facts of existence open up to an ultimate and pure fullness of being, unlimited by time and space. The thread we are following is leading us to what Johann Auer and Joseph Ratzinger have described as the "deep places of being" and an "enduring approach to the Ground of what is."[6] We detect evidence of order, and we reason to the existence of God and his life.

Here, the dominant culture casts philosophy and faith in a skeptical and suspicious shade. A strict and flat materialist would drearily and tediously reject these breathtaking truths. Saint Augustine said, "And men go out to admire the heights of mountains, the mighty waves of the sea, the vast tides of rivers, the course

---

5. Ibid., 209–215.
6. See Auer, Ratzinger, *Eschatology: Death and Eternal Life*, 24.

of the ocean, and the movements of the stars, and yet pass themselves by."[7] Saint Pope John Paul II said that the serious and humble scientist recognizes a complex immensity to reality that cannot be explained through scientific resources alone.[8] A purely materialistic science that truncates and dismisses the deeper questions is not cutting-edge but *cutting corners*, and very important ones at that. It cuts the thread and abandons reason's exploration of the mystery. The order of nature consists of much more than the merely material. It points to the order of grace, which builds on the order of nature. The true scientist is the believer who knows that the existence and movement of the universe, like that of the human bloodstream, simply cannot be reduced to the random collision of haphazard molecules at an arbitrary moment. As Pope Francis teaches: "Life is not the product of non-being or chance, but the fruit of a personal call and a personal love."[9]

Faith and reason

Faith is not pious guesswork as to the existence of God. Living faith actually *begins* with reason. Faith seeks out a deep-rooted knowledge surrounding facts that occur within history and existence. History and existence each point *beyond* themselves. They point with a compelling and convincing clarity to the supernatural action of God in time and space. The Church teaches that through the use of natural reason, we can know the existence of God with

---

7. *Confessions*, X, 8, 15. The author is grateful to Reverend Monsignor Ronny E. Jenkins for this translation.

8. See Saint John Paul II, *God: Father and Creator* as in *A Catechesis on the Creed* Volume 1 (Boston: Pauline Books & Media, 1996), 106–108.

9. *Lumen Fidei*, no. 11.

certainty on the basis of his works in the created world. The biblical authors knew well, as did every age of human history up to our own, that God's eternal reason is sensed in the power at work in creation.

The Book of Wisdom affirms this simple insight:

For all people who were ignorant of God were foolish by nature;
and they were unable from the good things that are seen to know the one who
exists, nor did they recognize the artisan while paying heed to his works. . . .
And if people were amazed at their power and working,
let them perceive from them
how much more powerful is the one who formed them.
For from the greatness and beauty of created things
comes a corresponding perception of their Creator. (Wis 13:1, 4–5)

Faith leads the believer straight through science, and science leads the scientist straight through faith. The prophet Amos sees through the natural to its supernatural cause and proclaims the wonders of "the one who made the Pleiades and Orion, and turns deep darkness into the morning, and darkens the day into night, who calls for the waters of the sea, and pours them out on the surface of the earth, the LORD is his name" (Amos 5:8–9). Saint Paul proclaims that God creates the world and the wonders of nature not simply to exist, but to be a path, "so that they would search for God and perhaps grope for him and find him—though indeed he is not far from each one of us" (Acts 17:27). Saint Paul emphasizes: "Ever since the creation of the world, his invisible attributes of eternal power and divinity have been able to be understood and perceived in what he has made" (Rom 1:20 NABRE).

Saint Paul does not refer to an imaginary world when he speaks of those invisible realities that God has made. The invisible is very real. For example, love is invisible, yet we can see the signs of love. In fact, love itself is more real than its signs. The back-and-forth exchange between the visible and invisible is one of the reasons the visible signs of authentic love are exciting and draw us always deeper into love. The interplay between the visible and the invisible is very important. Our natural reason leads us from those things that are seen to knowledge of unseen realities. On this very basis, Jesus calls us to see his works and to go deeper: "[E]ven though you do not believe me, believe the works [I do]" (Jn 10:38). This is why Saint Ignatius of Antioch, the second-century martyr, exhorted Saint Polycarp to "pray for the knowledge of things invisible."[10] God is invisible, immaterial, and incorporeal; this does not mean that he is abstract, theoretical, or impersonal.[11] Balthasar said, "Wherever his [God's] traces are seen in the world, mystery is involved."[12] The luminous vocation and deepest purpose of reason is to grope for God in his mystery. Reason thrives on mystery, especially that brilliant mysterious region that unites the *edge* of reason and the *beginning* of faith.

The beginning of faith

Yet, try as we might, we cannot, on the basis of natural reason alone, uncover the ultimate truth of the origin of our existence. We cannot capture God. While we can arrive at natural knowledge *that* God exists, only God himself could reveal himself as a personal, Triune God. We must be opened by grace to the absolutely free and generous self-disclosure of God. In his infinite, unbounded love

---

10. Saint Ignatius of Antioch, *Epistle of Ignatius to Polycarp,* Ch 2.
11. See Gabriel Bunge, *The Rublev Trinity* (New York: Saint Vladimir's Seminary Press), 1.
12. Hans Urs von Balthasar, *Theodrama II*, 53; see also *Theodrama IV*, 141.

God reached out to us in various ways throughout the Old Testament and ultimately through his only Son, who took on flesh and dwelt among us (see Jn 1:14). The Christian faith is not something people dreamed up through a blind projection of their fears into sentimental myth. It is quite the opposite. Faith begins and has its source in the light that comes forth from the living God, who calls out to us and reveals himself in unshakable love.[13] This love transforms us. The great Christian claim is that God has interacted with us and revealed himself not as an abstraction or mere presence, but as a personal being who has made himself known in limitless self-giving,[14] who acts intimately within history yet stands absolutely above it.

The Christian faith is a living response to the Triune God who has taken the initiative and drawn close to us. We are moved to believe not on the basis of our natural reason alone, but also on the basis of the authority of the God who freely reveals himself to us and manifests himself publicly in history. He stepped out of his eternity and proclaimed himself to Abraham. He spoke to Moses and proclaimed his name, "I AM WHO I AM" (Ex 3:14). He has spoken through the prophets. In the fullness of time his only-begotten Son "became flesh and lived among us, and we have seen his glory" (Jn 1:14). His only Son has made the Father known (see Jn 1:18; Heb 1:3; Col 1:15) and has shown us the full meaning of human existence. The light of living faith draws us to the free and deliberate act of faith as we observe the marvelous actions of God in history.

---

13. See *Lumen Fidei*, no. 4.
14. See Hans Urs von Balthasar, *Theodrama II*, 256.

—◦◦◦◦◦—

Chapter Seven

The Third Clue: Sin and Death

If we are created so wonderfully and we sense the infinite longing deep in our hearts, and if existence is so multifaceted and mysterious, then *why death*? Can our journey through this troubling maze to understand death and loss only lead us in circles?

Death: Is God the culprit?

It is a modern temptation to think that we can hastily figure out God and then neatly dismiss him. This is a common temptation for the modern mind. We think we are intellectually sophisticated, but we readily admit we have little room for any mystery that cannot be resolved in less than five minutes. If it takes too long we begin to panic, demand a way out and attack the mystery we cannot understand: God. We may accuse God of being an unconcerned rule-maker or an absent superstition. We think that the all-powerful, all-knowing, and all-loving God should do everything *we* want. And we don't want the pain of death.

Ironically, the caricature of a temperamental, rule-obsessed, control-based being describes human beings, not God. It is we who, under the burden of sin, become the tyrant.

To the popular mindset, God is three, simultaneously irreconcilable things. First, he knows everything perfectly, so he knows when death is approaching. Second, he is all-good and all-loving, so he must not want death. Third, he is all-powerful, so he has the power to stop death in its tracks. Yet, *death is*. The atheist and agnostic find it easy to reason through this dilemma. The fact of death seems to negate God's goodness, knowledge, and might. And maybe, just maybe, the atheist contends, the fact of death cancels God himself. The case seems closed.

For people today, God's knowledge, goodness, and power trip over one another and conflict. If God had perfect knowledge, he would know in advance when bad things will happen. If he were all-loving, he would want to stop bad things from happening. If he were all-powerful, he would be able stop bad things from happening. But bad things do happen. Then God has all those arbitrary rules. It seems he won't lift a finger to stop a devastating earthquake, but he will wreak relentless havoc on sinners. So people today think that if God exists at all, he is a rule-obsessed, erratic leftover from the Middle Ages who is still trying to manipulate a world that left him behind long ago.

It is rather convenient to make God out to be the culprit as far as death is concerned. His fingerprints seem to be all over death. It would seem that either God is the cause of death and not good, or that God is good and death is stronger than God. But, the ancient and inspired insight of the Book of Wisdom firmly testifies otherwise: "God did not make death, and he does not delight in the death of the living. For he created all things so that they might exist" (Wis 1:13–14). The Prophet Ezekiel shares this time-tested understanding: he tells us that God takes no pleasure in death and that the Lord does not want the sinner to die (see Ez 18:23). The Prophet Joel boldly proclaims the beautiful truth that God is relenting in punishment (see Jl 2:13). The witness of Scripture is firm: death is not God-made. So it seems that God is not the convenient villain some would make him out to be. Why then, in such a beautiful world called into being by a merciful God, does death exist?

Death as fashioned by human hands

It seems our thread has led us up to a blank wall or, worse, a treacherous cliff that drops into a bottomless ravine. Or perhaps we have been staring the answer in the face. Perhaps the thread leads to a mirror. Up to now we have not questioned the one remaining suspect: human beings. What if death was brought about by the choice of human beings?

God is the very first one to speak about death in Scripture. He tells the first man: "You are free to eat from any of the trees of the garden except the tree of knowledge of good and evil. From that tree you shall not eat; when you eat from it you shall die" (Gn 2:16–17). All-knowing and all-good, God is not threatening the man with death, but warning him where danger lies. God tells him the truth. God tells the man that it is possible for him to die, and he counsels him on how to avoid that danger. The forbidden tree does not restrict the man, but allows him freedom. He is free to enjoy the entire garden. The prohibition on the tree serves to remind the man that he has a special and unique relationship with God; he depends on God as his very origin. The man must live by the word of God.

But an opposing voice pronounces a separate opinion: "You will not die; for God knows that when you eat of it [the tree in the middle of the Garden] your eyes will be opened, and you will be like God, knowing good and evil" (Gn 3:4–5). This sinister whisper suggests to our first parents that there is no death. Behind the menacing suggestion lurks a deeper drive: "Lead them to focus their attention not on the fact that the generous God has given them the entire garden save for one tree. Rather, direct them to focus exclusively on the one thing that is not theirs." Satan spins the tale that the bountiful and generous God is really unreasonably strict and severe.[1]

God wished the human race to remain free from sin. Our bond with God was founded on our creation in God's image and likeness. Prior to his sin, the first man lived in a state of original innocence and walked in harmony with God. Yet, being created in the image and likeness of God came with some risk. As we have seen, since we are created in the image of God who is infinite, we experience a longing for the infinite. Although our longing is for the infinite, we ourselves are not infinite. As creatures, we are finite, dependent on the constant address of God. The first man hears all of this in the murmur: "You will not die; for God knows that when you eat of it [the tree in the middle of the Garden] your eyes will be opened, and you will be like God, knowing good and evil" (Gn 3:4–5).

". . . [W]hen you eat of it your eyes will be opened . . ." These words are the hinge of the temptation of original sin. As he utters them, Satan tells the man at least two things. First, Satan tells him that his infinite longing does not come from God, but from *his own self*. Second, Satan tells him that only the man can fulfill his infinite longing *by himself and on his own terms*. To this the devil adds the deadly mixture of ambition and fear: ambition in that the day the man eats of the tree, he will be like God; fear in saying, "You will not die," which implies not eating of the tree will lead to death. Satan suggests that the man is to be God's *equal* (ambition) and that God

---

1. Hans Urs von Balthasar, *The Christian State of Life* (San Francisco: Ignatius Press, 2002), 90.

is the man's *enemy* (fear). At the heart of every temptation the devil seeks to replace faith with fear. Satan, "the deceiver of the whole world" (Rev 12:9), lures us into fearing that God, in his own time, will not fill our infinite yearning. Our own contingency then becomes a threat to us, a frustratingly desperate state that we must conquer. The devil, the liar from the beginning (see Jn 8:44), does all of this by portraying God as lying to us. We are tempted to stop trusting that God will be enough. The marrow of the original temptation, and every temptation since, lies here. Satan simply stands alongside our infinite longing and holds up a mirror. We look into the mirror and see into eternity on our own terms. The dark illusion begins to spread.

Original sin: the fault lines

The deeper subterranean fault lines of the temptation are clear. The temptation arises at the intersection of Adam's infinite capacity and his contingency. Satan tries to convince him that the freedom God gives is not freedom but oppression. The devil, in his calculated malice, seduces the man *to take the cry for the infinite into his own hands*. Everything hangs on the lie, "you will be like gods." Why is this statement a lie? They *already were like God*, created in his image and likeness. The devil wants Adam to reject there being created in God's image by convincing them being like God is simply not enough, and Adam can do better on his own. Thus, our first parents are tempted to pride, to pretend that they can fill this infinite depth *on their own*.

Pride, that most basic of deceptions, reduces everything to a purely earthly level. The sad strategy is to convince Adam to treat himself and not God as infinite. The temptation is designed to turn Adam's inherent orientation to God back on himself. In attempting to absolutize himself, the man denies *both* himself and God. Original sin, fueled by pride, is a sin of disobedience by which man denies God's infinitude and his own finitude, and attempts to exchange one for the other. And so, at the very beginning of human history Adam made the disastrous choice: he disobeyed God and rejected God's will. But as a finite being, he cannot fulfill his infinite longing. The temptation sounded so attractive with its promise of self-sufficiency. But the finite is not self-sufficient. Why did the man want to be self-sufficient? The motivation was prideful self-love. Saint Thomas explains that self-love is the cause of every sin.[2] But a finite creature must always freely turn its will in obedience to its Creator, to God. As already noted, God enabled the first man and woman to do this by the gift of habitual sanctifying grace in the state of original innocence. Through this habitual grace, they enjoyed supernatural gifts. Only in this obedient and gifted, grace-filled turn toward God is there no sin. The devil is the first to suggest that complete, loving obedience to God is opposed to authentic freedom. Until then, the response of faithful obedience to their Creator had galvanized and preserved our first parents in the state of original innocence with the gifts of sanctifying grace.[3]

Original sin is aimed at the deepest place of human identity and dignity. As discussed earlier, the human person is the image and likeness of God due to the faculties associated with intellect and will. It is exactly this rationality and freedom that the devil incites the man to use against God. "Within the context of God's creative gift we can best see the essence of the first sin—man's free choice made with a misuse of these faculties."[4] Adam freely

---

2. See *Summa Theologiae* Ia, q 77, *sed contra*.

3. See Hans Urs von Balthasar, *The Christian State of Life*, 93.

4. Saint John Paul II, *Jesus, Son and Savior: A Catechesis on the Creed, Vol. II* (Boston: Pauline Books & Media, 1996), 23.

decided to disobey God's command and to attempt to fill the infinite yearning for the absolute, residing at the center of his being, with his own passing and finite existence. Original sin is thus a terrible knot, the primordial event involving the free and deliberate choice to disobey God and to reject his command. Original sin marks the first time that man opposed God, and in doing so he sinned gravely. As the Second Vatican Council teaches, "from the very onset of his history man abused his liberty."[5] Man, a creature, freely chose to do something incompatible with God, his Creator. Man did evil.

The very moment the creature turns away in disobedience from its Creator and toward itself the temptation vanishes with nothing left except the hollow, resonating sin. The man allowed the devil's temptation to reverberate in the interior part of his soul; his reason was darkened and he freely chose to sin. In doing so he destroys his original obedience. His free obedience was the life-giving channel that allowed him to grasp, trust, and participate directly and deeply in the link between the order of nature and the order of grace. The fundamental evil of sin sent a seismic shockwave into the man's deepest places. It necessarily caused a deep fracture and deformation in his heart the very moment it was committed. Immediately, by his own choice and decision, Adam lost the holiness and justice in which he had been created. Therefore the effects were immediate. He freely committed original sin—and God does not override human freedom. By pushing away from God, who is infinite, Adam tried to be his own infinite source and goal. The only logical result is that he then fell. When Adam rejected God and sinned, at once he fell from the state of justice and holiness. Yet, the image of God in

---

5. *Gaudium et Spes,* no. 13.

the human person, and our infinite longing, though marred by sin, remain in us.

It is important to emphasize that the one who sinned, Adam, the first man, is not just any man. In a sense he is the "founder" or "representative" of the entire human race.[6] As such, his sin affected the entire human race. By his sinful disobedience he immediately forfeited the grace of original innocence and the sanctifying grace by which he possessed supernatural gifts. As Saint Paul teaches, "Therefore, just as sin came into the world through one man, and death came through sin, and so death spread to all because all have sinned" (Rom 5:12). The Church teaches, therefore, that the effects of original sin are universal and are passed on by this sin's hereditary character.

God describes the consequences of this dreadful sin:

> And to the man he said, "Because you have listened to the voice of your wife, and have eaten of the tree about which I commanded you, 'You shall not eat of it,' cursed is the ground because of you; in toil you shall eat of it all the days of your life; thorns and thistles it shall bring forth for you; and you shall eat the plants of the field. By the sweat of your face you shall eat bread until you return to the ground, for out of it you were taken; you are dust, and to dust you shall return." (Gn 3:17–19)

Adam's offense against God burdens the entire human race with a continuous struggle in both body and soul. We experience disorder in our senses and appetites, our will is weakened, and our reason is darkened. The order of nature does not cease to exist. It is, however, deeply wounded and we find it exceedingly difficult to perceive the order of grace. As the *Catechism of the Catholic Church* teaches:

---

6. See Saint John Paul II, *Jesus, Son and Savior*, 28.

"After that first sin, the world is virtually inundated by sin" (*CCC* 401). We are subject to futility (see Rom 8:20ff.). Daily life is governed by the law of the jungle. We are repeatedly tempted to turn pleasure and self-satisfaction into an idol. We are easily and subtly tangled up in our own ego and drive for power. The constant pull toward self-interest seems inescapable. Our lot is one of alienation, struggle, and sorrow. We are more easily tempted to forget God. And, of course, we know now that constant burden: death. Since the way to life comes only through God, when we reach out to something other than God, we choose death over life (see Gn 2:17; 3:19). With original sin, "Death makes its entrance into human history," (*CCC* 4000). Death is the consequence of original sin in the same way that falling is the consequence of stepping off a cliff. We experience death because of sin, not because death is somehow natural to human nature. To learn more about the mystery of death we must look more closely at the mystery of sin.

The sin of the fallen angels

God did not make death. Sin did. God also did not make human sin. Man did. No sin is natural to us. The first man committed original sin, but sin itself did not begin with him. Nor did sin arise in his path as an arbitrary pitfall. Sin itself began with Satan. Sin arose as part of a strategy by which evil assaults the human race. As with every temptation since then, the first temptation to sin was cleverly designed (see Gn 3:1) to make us *doubt* God. On the basis of this doubt the devil incites the human person to freely contradict, oppose, and reject God as the sole source of all goodness. The devil does not incite us directly at first. If he approached us directly we would quickly catch sight of his evil and flee him. Instead he uses a strategy: temptation. The devil always makes temptation sound and look good. It always begins with an indirect nudge. At first, the devil hides behind the things of the world, such as power and pleasure, and uses them as masks to disguise his approach.[7] He prods us to indulge, to cut a small corner, or to take a few extra dollars from the petty cash box. He strokes our ego. H. M. Féret, O.P., calls our attention to how insidious the tempter is: "At first we almost fail to recognize him . . . He insinuates himself unobtrusively, slyly, calling no attention to himself. Only toward the end does he throw off the mask, permitting us to catch a glimpse of his hatred and ill-will."[8] Why does the devil tempt us? Saint Pope John Paul II recounts the teaching that human sin is a "reflection and consequence" of the sin that had already taken place "in the world of invisible beings."[9] This world of invisible beings is the angelic world. Since they are rational creatures, angels could sin. Sacred Scripture speaks of those angels "who did not keep their own position, but left their proper dwelling," whom God has kept "in eternal chains in deepest darkness for the judgment of the great day" (Jd 1:6). Saint Peter reminds us that "God did not spare the angels when they sinned" (2 Pt 2:4).

The devil began his existence as an angel named Lucifer. Angels are pure spirits, invisible, rational creatures created by God. Saint Thomas tells us that as pure spirits, angels occupy a distinguished rank above that of bodily beings, including human beings, in relation to God.[10] Lucifer was given the task to administer the material beauty of the visible universe.[11] Since light illuminates beauty,

7. See Louis Bouyer, *The Spirituality of the New Testament and the Fathers* (New York: Desclee Company, 1960), 310.

8. H. M. Féret, O.P., *The Apocalypse of St. John* (Maryland: The Newman Press, 1958), 113.

9. Saint John Paul II, *Jesus, Son and Savior*, 30.

10. See *STh* Ia, q 50, a1, ad 1.

11. See Jean Daniélou, *The Angels and Their Mission: According to the Fathers of the Church*, trans. David Heimann (Westminster, MD: Newman Press, 1957), 46.

Lucifer's name means "bearer of light." Indeed, Saint Thomas tells us that Lucifer surpassed all the hosts of the angels in brightness.[12] In his angelic knowledge, Lucifer foresaw that something would take place in the history of the visible world, something which he in his pride could simply not abide. He foresaw that the Son of God, the second Person of the Blessed Trinity, would take human nature, the nature of flesh, in the Incarnation. In his conceit Lucifer understood this as a rebuff, that the Son would bypass the pure spirit status of angelic nature to take the nature of flesh. "[Lucifer] revolted because he could not endure that man should be more loved than himself."[13] Pride, his own self-love, became the source of his hatred for God by which Lucifer opposed God's plan. By his sin of original pride, Lucifer was cast down from heaven, as sacred Scripture testifies:

> How you are fallen from heaven,
>   O Day Star, son of Dawn!
> How you are cut down to the ground,
>   you who laid the nations low!
> You said in your heart,
>   I will ascend to heaven;
> I will raise my throne
>   above the stars of God;

---

12. See *Summa Theologiae* Ia, q 63, a7, *sed contra*.

13. Jean Daniélou, *Holy Pagans of the Old Testament*, Felix Faber, trans. (New York: Longman's, Green and Co, 1956), 37; see also Jean Daniélou, *The Angels and Their Mission*, 45–47. See Louis Bouyer, *The Meaning of the Monastic Life* (New York: P.J. Kennedy and Sons, 1955), 30–32. See also Gabriel Bunge, OSB, *Dragon's Wine and Angel's Bread: The Teaching of Evagrius Ponticus on Anger and Meekness* (New York: St. Vladimir's Seminary Press, 2009), 29–31. Note that while Saint Thomas teaches that the angels do not know future events, he affirms that in their superior intelligence they do discern in a more distinct and perfect way the succession of future events that proceed from knowable causes (See *STh* Ia, q 57 a 3).

I will sit on the mount of assembly
    on the heights of Zaphon;
I will ascend to the tops of the clouds,
    I will make myself like the Most High."
But you are brought down to Sheol,
    to the depths of the Pit. (Is 14:12–15)[14]

Saint Paul likewise tells us that pride was the sin of Lucifer (see 1 Tim 3:6). Saint Thomas Aquinas agrees.[15]

The mission of the angels is to give glory to God and to make known the mysteries of God's reign. Saint Thomas teaches that in order to carry out their mission, the angels are to converse with human beings as intellectual companions.[16] Although Lucifer is cast down from this mission, he still converses with us. Instead of leading us to give glory to God, Lucifer tempts us to the very same sin of pride by which he rejected God's plan. Lucifer, the devil, does this out of envy. Since he destroyed his own relationship with God, the fallen angel does not want us to have a relationship with God either. This is what envy does. It seeks to destroy the good of another person. Hence, the devil's envy is his motive for inducing us to sin and therefore to death: "through the devil's envy death entered the world" (Wis 2:24). The devil knew that if we were to sin and reject God, then we would reap the bitter fruit of death.

The *Catechism of the Catholic Church* reminds us that the devil does not have infinite power (*CCC* 395). He remains a powerful pure spirit and has attained a particular dominance over us, even though we remain free (*CCC* 407). As Saint John tells us: "We know that we are God's children, and that the whole world lies under the power of

---

14. See also Job 4:18; and *STh* Ia, q 63, *sed contra*.
15. See *Summa Theologiae* Ia, q 63, a 2.
16. See *Summa Theologiae* Ia, q 51, a2, ad 1.

the evil one" (1 Jn 5:19). Nonetheless, the devil is still a creature. In his hatred for God the devil attacks us and creation so as to cause not only grave spiritual injury, but also physical injury, even if indirectly (see Jb 1:18–19). Saint Peter therefore exhorts us, "Discipline yourselves, keep alert. Like a roaring lion your adversary the devil prowls around, looking for someone to devour" (1 Pet 5:8). In inducing us to sin, the devil used death in his attempt to destroy us. We harm ourselves greatly when we disobey God. *But God does not harm us.* In fact, God longs to come to our rescue.

The Protoevangelium

Each verse, indeed every word of Sacred Scripture has unfathomable depth. The words that God speaks immediately after the commission of original sin are especially profound, but we can easily miss their significance. After Adam and Eve sin, God says to the devil, "Because you have done this, cursed are you among all animals and among all wild creatures; upon your belly you shall go, and dust you shall eat all the days of your life" (Gn 3:14). God further says, "I will put enmity between you and the woman, and between your offspring and hers; he will strike your head, and you will strike his heel" (Gn 3:15). God does not make threats. *He makes promises.* The promise God makes is known as the *Protoevangelium*, a word that means "the first proclamation of the Gospel."[17]

Notice the utterly profound depths of God's immediate response to the first sin. God does not rant and rave, nor does he

---

17. The great promise of God is echoed in the Suffering Servant song of the prophet Isaiah (Is 53:11–12; Mt 20:28; Jn 8:34–36; Acts 3:16); she is also foretold as the Virgin who will conceive and bear a son, whose name will be Emmanuel (Is 7:14); cf. Second Vatican Council, *Lumen Gentium*, 55.

abandon or desert the human race. The very first thing God says is that he *has a plan*. He announces his wise and loving plan to send the Savior. God promises a coming victory. God's saving plan begins to unfold immediately after the Fall. He speaks at once of the enmity between Satan and the woman, and between her offspring and the devil. Saint Pope John Paul II points out that God "makes the woman the first 'enemy' of the prince of darkness."[18] The "woman" mentioned here is our Lady, the Blessed Virgin Mary, the first to benefit from the victory of Jesus. The "enmity" is the battle between evil and the Lord that began and unfolds throughout history. Saint Paul speaks of this battle when he says, "For our struggle is not against enemies of blood and flesh, but against the rulers, against the authorities, against the cosmic powers of this present darkness, against the spiritual forces of evil in the heavenly places" (Eph 6:12). The Second Vatican Council likewise affirms, "A monumental struggle against the powers of darkness pervades the whole history of man. The battle was joined from the very origins of the world and will continue until the last day."[19]

The connection between sin and death

That death is a consequence of sin can sound harsh. But a deeper element is at work in the mystery of death. God says, "Now, what if he [man] also reaches out his hand to take fruit from the tree of life, and eats of it and lives forever?" (Gn 3:22). If man were to reach out to the tree of life, he would live forever in the state of alienation from God. God then banishes man from paradise, "stationing the cherubim and the fiery revolving sword east of the garden of Eden,

---

18. Saint John Paul II, *Jesus, Son and Savior*, 81.
19. *Gaudium et Spes,* no. 37.

to guard the way to the tree of life" (Gn 3:24). But this exile from paradise is not condemnation to permanent anguish. Von Balthasar recalls the tradition that the revolving flaming sword bore the likeness of mother and child.[20] Even as he banishes the first couple from paradise, God's promise is *already unfolding.* The consequences of sin are not aspects of a stubborn revenge but a way that the sinful state in which Adam and Eve had entangled themselves *might not be made permanent.* Without death, the curse of sin would only *intensify.* God has made a promise. He intends to lead humanity back to the tree of life by another path.

God also *explains* to Adam and Eve the consequences they have brought upon themselves. God says, "By the sweat of your face you shall eat bread until you return to the ground, for out of it you were taken; you are dust, and to dust you shall return" (Gn 3:19). Physical death is the ultimate temporal consequence of the sin they have committed. They have brought down the penalties on themselves as a natural consequence of their freely chosen action. They are the authors of their own sentence.

To say that death is a consequence of sin does not necessarily mean that a person who dies today does so as the immediate effect of a specific personal sin (see Lk 13:1–5; Jn 9:2–3). The connection goes far deeper. At the time of creation, God gave the human race dominion over the visible world (see Gn 1:28). They had this original dominion because they also had preternatural gifts, which enhanced their natural abilities. They lived in harmony with creation and knew more clearly the mysteries of the natural world. Hurricanes, tornadoes, and earthquakes may still have occurred, but perhaps human beings could have lived in concord even with these. Prior to sin, integral human nature enhanced by the preternatural gifts could have

---

20. See Hans Urs von Balthasar, *The Christian State of Life*, 122.

included the capacity to discern very early the natural signs of these events, so that their beauty was manifested and no harm done. With the preternatural gifts, we would have been able to deal with many of the earthly things that we now call upon God to "fix."

Recall the horrendous Indonesian tsunami of 2004. It did not strike because of an individual's personal sin. God was not taking cosmic revenge for an infraction. Interestingly, the animals in a large wildlife preserve had all migrated to higher ground long before their island was hit by the catastrophic wall of water. Reportedly, only two of the wildlife in the preserve perished.[21] This may seem coincidental or a fluke, but could something deeper account for that remarkable fact? Could their natural survival instinct have so connected them to the physical world that they could pick up natural signs of the looming disaster? People saw signs of the tsunami only as it was about to strike. By sin, we forfeited and lost the preternatural gifts. Now we earn our living by the sweat of our brow (see Gn 3:19), and have had to work hard for this knowledge through scientific discoveries.

And so, on the basis of repeated tests and experiments, researchers today can point to hazardous substances, foods, and other man-made agents that may cause cancer, heart disease, or other ill effects. Experts readily admit that there is much we do not know about the many chemicals and other substances we create and use. Over time, the harmful ingredients may affect even our genetics and heredity, posing future risks to our children. Poor diet, lack of physical exercise, and other negative lifestyle choices reflect the struggle of the appetites and the weakening of our reason and will. Perhaps, prior to sin, our gifted harmony with creation included a much

---

21. See http://news.nationalgeographic.com/news/2005/01/0104_050104_tsunami_animals_2.html.

more advanced intuition and resistance to what would be otherwise physically dangerous for us.

In the wake of a natural disaster or a tragic accident, we can very quickly blame God. In light of the above, we may more clearly grasp that our objections are really complaints *against ourselves* for the original loss of the preternatural gifts.

God did not create death. Nor does God create those things that directly cause death, such as cancer and disease. Disease and death are evils. God is all good and all he creates is good. So God cannot be the cause of evil. That which God does *not* cause *must* be the cause of evil. The only thing God does not cause is *nothing*. Evil is *a privation or lack of a good that should be present and is not*. Understood in this way, evil is a lack, a privation of the good. This is a crucial point for us to understand when we feel like blaming God for the painful things that happen to us. In no place does the Gospel tell us that the world itself is evil, but the Gospel does tell us that "the whole world lies under the power of the evil one" (1 Jn 5:19).[22] God does not cause the privation. The sin that we commit as individuals—or the often unforeseen effects of the sins of those who have gone before us—does.[23]

Death's deeper secret

Death is a moment unlike any other. Death teaches the human race the lesson it once disobediently rejected in Eden: that only God is infinite; human beings are finite. Everything we should have learned from birth we must now, after sin, learn completely through

---

22. See Henri DeLubac, *A Brief Catechesis on Nature and Grace*, 166.

23. See *STh* Ia, q 75, a1; see also Hans Urs von Balthasar, *Theodrama Theological Dramatic Theory I: Prologomena* (San Francisco: Ignatius Press, 1988), 48.

death. Death demonstrates in clear terms that we are *not* the source and center of life. Since we refused the other signs of our finitude, death necessarily becomes its ultimate herald. Death finally persuades us of the fragile limit of our mistaken self-sufficiency and the utter falsehood of our self-centeredness. Death proves irrefutably that we are not autonomous. Seen in this light, death *redirects* us to live life as we truly are, finite. Death is the unmistakable moment when our finitude brushes up against God's infinity.

The day, the hour, and the moment eventually comes that cannot be covered by any human insurance. In that moment all we have done and accumulated simply fails, falls away, and collapses. No matter how impressive our résumés, how notable our achievements, or how grand our reputations, we cannot escape death. Our worldly possessions, expertise, and accomplishments cannot give us a reprieve once we die. Jesus tells his disciples the parable of the man who piled up tremendous wealth and built barns to hold all of his possessions. The Lord calls this man a *fool*: "You fool! This very night your life is being demanded of you. And the things you have prepared, whose will they be?" (Lk 12:20; see also Ps 39:6–7).

As death demonstrates our finitude, it also teaches us finally to listen to the abiding and overwhelming truth that we are meant for more, for the Infinite, for God. Our finitude means more than that we will die. In its other, *more primary* and positive meaning, finitude points to an *openness*. In fact, our finitude is not so much that we have an end to this earthly life, but that we are creatures in the midst of our earthly existence. The dependence and yearning at the heart of our existence are not signs of the weakness of human nature, but of its incredible value.

In addition to the moment of conception, two of the most mysterious moments of human existence in the visible world are the moment of birth and the moment of death. We ask relatively few questions about birth, about where we come from, and most of these are biological questions. But our origins are deeper than simple biology. If we are satisfied only with surface answers about conception and birth, we are more than likely *missing* the point of life. The same is true of questions about death. If we stop simply at the biological data, we are missing the *point* of death.

In death, the corpse reminds us, on a natural level, of our ultimate contingency and dependence. Our natural contingency is a clue and sign of God. The experience of birth and death allow us to peer with alarming clarity into the infinite. As we grow, we recognize with greater awareness that our existence has a deep meaning that even the most notable accomplishments cannot fulfill. We awaken to and begin to recognize a deeper and elusive connection: we did not cause ourselves and we cannot, on our own, fulfill ourselves. The ground of our being is utterly beyond us. At birth and at death the *metaphysical*, which is present to us every day, unmistakably breaks through.[24] By *metaphysical* I do not mean the ambiguous and "enlightened" new age subculture. Rather, by metaphysical I refer to the classical transcendent nature of being itself, and God who reveals himself in history.

When death introduces us to our contingency, our contingency begins to introduce us again to God. Sin alienates us from God, but God continues to call to us. God seeks to guide us back to himself by his plan of redemption. The Prophet Hosea tells us that when we forget God, he says of our soul, "I will hedge in her way with thorns and erect a wall against her so that she cannot find her paths. . . . I

---

24. See Johann Auer and Joseph Ratzinger, *Dogmatic Theology 9: Eschatology Death and Eternal Life* (Washington, D.C.: The Catholic University of America Press, 1988), 70. Henri De Lubac, SJ, pointed out the common opinion that death "is the only metaphysical experience" see his *The Drama of Atheist Humanism* (San Francisco: Ignatius Press, 1995), 393.

will allure her now; I will lead her into the desert and speak persuasively to her" (Hos 2:8, 16 NABRE). When I touched the dead man's hand as I passed his coffin, something happened to me. I touched the thread of the *no more*. On that afternoon, I touched the contingency of which death reminds us all. The body of the Christian, even in death, is a symbol of something more. So when I touched the man's still, lifeless hand, it touched something within reality and within me. I touched a corpse, but I did *more* than touch a corpse. I grasped, or rather, was grasped by a *clue*.

In this earthly life the body of the Christian is a temple of the Holy Spirit. Saint Pope John Paul II taught that "through the fact that the Word of God became flesh the body entered theology . . . through the main door."[25] In death the body retains its dignity. The body of the deceased Christian is a sign. This is why we treat the remains with reverence and bury the body in hallowed ground. In touching the dead man's hand, I had *touched* a sign of hope in the resurrection. Von Balthasar reminds us that touch is the most fundamental and unerring of the senses.[26] In feeling other things, living things *also feel themselves*. As Adrienne von Speyr says: "When a living man touches a dead man, this always expresses much more than when he touches someone who is still alive. In his touch lies something of a form of address, a bequest. . . ."[27] As I touched that hand *I was handed* a clue: the corpse of a Christian points to the resurrection. I couldn't let go of the clue. I was changed, not because of that man, or my own inquisitiveness, but because of Jesus Christ.

---

25. Saint John Paul II, *Man and Woman He Created Them* (Boston: Pauline Books & Media, 2006), 221.

26. See Balthasar, *The Glory of the Lord I*, 339, 394.

27. Adrienne von Speyr, *Mark: Meditations on the Gospel of Mark*, trans. Michelle Borras (San Francisco: Ignatius Press, 2012), 259.

Christ had used that Christian man's body as an *instrument* to lead all who paid their respects deeper into the mystery of eternal life. Attending a wake or funeral is a polite expression of condolence, but it is also an opportunity to pray for the salvation of the deceased, that the merits of Christ's sacrifice may be applied in their fullness. As we do so, the body of the Christian, even in death, is meant to be transformed into a witness to the victory of Christ. Thus the thread we hold now converges directly into the path of God's plan of redemption carried out by his only begotten Son, our Lord Jesus Christ.

CHAPTER EIGHT

Jesus and Death: God's Own Tears

Magic, mystery, and miracles

As I stood outside the funeral home at the age of ten, I was afraid. When my mom died two years later, I was very afraid. I was afraid of living without the daily experience of her love. When we lose love we have two options: fear or deeper love. We rarely admit our fear, and we don't immediately turn to deeper love when we have lost someone. Fear becomes our path for awhile.

After my mother's death, I wanted God to step in and, like a magic trick, wave his hand and turn everything back to normal. I thought God's power was the power of magic. That's a common mistake. I did not consciously think that God was magical, but I wanted it to be true. In times of pain we can think that since God is God, he should do everything immediately, completely, and in an awe-inspiring way. In such moments, we want him to be a God of magical outcomes. In addition to the big losses, we face many daily losses, such as a friend moving away, a job change, or simply getting lost on the highway. Even in these daily losses, we can choose love or fear. In our fear, we get into the habit of expecting God to fix even minor problems quickly. Fear tempts us to want God to be magical.

For all of its allure, magic has no *mystery*. Magic is an illusion that invites superficial attention. Mystery, on the other hand, invites the whole person into its truthful depths. In fact, when God insists that he is *not* a God of magic, rather than following him into his mystery, we rush to the odd "magic" of anger. When God doesn't wave his hand and fix things, we turn our backs and try to fix *him*. The temptation to seek magic solutions can trick us into thinking that the human being, not God, is in control of everything. Of course, no reasonable person believes in magic, but many very reasonable people believe in *control*. Where there is control there is always fear. Fear does two things to bring about a reaction of control: Fear hides and it rushes. Hiding and rushing are fear's magical attempts to control an unsafe world. Hiding can be exciting for children who play hide and seek, but adults also hide, often right out in the open. Some hide in drugs, in excessive work, or in front of a computer screen. Others hide behind a fancy car, or through name dropping, or having the last word. And rushing about may not always be the result of a busy person's demanding pace. Fear-based rushing in a hectic, internal world may cause one to be always on the move to the next proof of his or her own value. Hence rushing can mask high perfectionistic expectations and an ongoing attempt to be accepted and to please others. We can hide and rush for a very long time.

It often takes years to learn that God is not a God of magic. He is *infinitely more*. God is a God of *love*. This means he is a God of mystery. Love is not magic but hard work. Yes, falling in love can take only a moment, but *learning* to love takes a long time, for it is a splendid mystery. One of the most astounding mysteries is that God's love doesn't give up even when we do. He is a God of love and his "perfect love casts out fear" (1 Jn 4:18). The temptation to want

God to fix things automatically is a very strong one. But God never tires of waiting to lead us into his mystery and his love. He does not force us, or control us—because love does not force or control. Love invites. Love invites us to let go of our expectation that God be magical, and to take another step into his mystery.

And part of God's mystery are his miracles. A miracle contains not an ounce of magic. Miracles are not divine tricks that give God the last word in difficult situations. Miracles aren't about outcomes—they are about Jesus Christ, the only Son of God. And so miracles are full of mystery. They are not ends in themselves. They are mighty wonders that God works, such as healing or wielding a power over nature, which can only be credited to divine action. The miracles that God worked in the Old Testament were a sign of his promise to send a Savior. The miracles that Jesus worked in the New Testament were signs that Jesus is the Messiah and that the Kingdom of God was breaking through. Miracles point to the divinity of Jesus. They also point us back to the small, mysterious, and sacred moments in which God reveals his love.

In his public ministry, Jesus begins to announce the fulfillment of the mysterious saving plan of God. His entire mission is to confront sin and death. Yet, the Lord encounters death directly on at least three occasions. He meets those who tell him of the death of the daughter of Jairus, that of the son of the widow of Nain, and that of his friend Lazarus. Each passage recounts how the Lord encounters death and those who mourn. In these events worked by the Lord's power, the dead persons return to earthly life. Each would die again later. The Lord does not perform these signs to force people to believe in him with a compelling display of his own power. The miraculous is not magical. Rather, the Lord's miraculous raising of the dead is a sign that he is the Messiah (see Lk 7:22–23; Mt 11:4–5). He "links the resurrection to his own person. . . . Already now, in this present life he gives us a sign and pledge of this by restoring the dead to life, announcing this own Resurrection, though it was to be of another order."[1] These accounts are also important for our own meditation as they lead us more deeply into the mystery of Jesus and God's saving plan.

Jairus' daughter

> While he was saying these things to them, suddenly a leader of the synagogue came in and knelt before him, saying, "My daughter has just died; but come and lay your hand on her, and she will live." And Jesus got up and followed him, with his disciples. . . . When Jesus came to the leader's house and saw the flute players and the crowd making a commotion, he said, "Go away; for the girl is not dead but sleeping." And they laughed at him. But when the crowd had been put outside, he went in and took her by the hand, and the girl got up. And the report of this spread throughout that district. (Mt 9:18–19, 23–26; see Mk 5:21–24, 35–43, and Lk 8:40–42; 49–56)

Jesus attended wakes too. The first time was for a young girl, the daughter of a synagogue official, whom Saint Mark and Saint Luke tell us was named Jairus. As a synagogue official, Jairus leads a busy life filled with demands. One day he learns his daughter is deathly ill, so he comes to Jesus and shows him homage by falling at his feet and presenting his urgent petition. He pleads with Jesus to come and heal his dying daughter. Saint Matthew tells us the situation is far worse: the official tells the Lord that his daughter has already died. The word Saint Matthew uses for death is not the usual Greek word, *apothnēskō*, but *teleutaō*, meaning finished or completed. This same word, *teleutaō*, is the word the Lord himself will speak from the cross when he cries out, "It is finished!" (Jn 19:30). Already, the encounter of Jairus and Jesus is connected to the death of the Lord.

---

1. *CCC* 994; see also, Saint John Paul II, *Jesus, Son and Savior*, 498.

Jairus asks Jesus to come to his house and touch his child so that the young girl will come to life again. In each of the accounts, Jesus, without saying a word, immediately follows the official. Notice the Lord's humility. The Gospel has told us that Jairus is a leader, and now Jesus allows Jairus to lead him. After Jairus finishes speaking the Gospel tells us that "Jesus got up and followed him . . ." (Mt 9:19). The Greek word used here for "arose," *egeirō*, is the same word used to describe the resurrection of Jesus on Easter morning (see Jn 21:14). Every action of the Lord is filled with hope.

The accounts in the Gospel of Mark and of Luke, in which the official asks Jesus to come and heal his sick daughter, carry an added significance. As Jesus is on his way to the house of Jairus, a messenger arrives with the devastating report that the young girl has died. He tells Jairus not to bother Jesus any further.

This sad moment deepens the mystery in several ways. First, all three Gospel accounts are now in agreement. Those who have examined the daughter assert that she is dead; her death is beyond dispute. Second, a mysterious, unnamed messenger brings news of the child's death. Third, this messenger also seeks to turn Jesus back. Perhaps the messenger was only trying to be courteous, so as not to interrupt Jesus further. Jairus had summoned Jesus to heal the girl, but that is now impossible. On a deeper level, however, we note that the anonymous messenger is the opposite of Jairus. In the face of death, Jairus seeks out Jesus, does him homage, and invites him to his home. In the very same situation the messenger seeks out Jesus, does not pay him homage, and *uninvites* Jesus. This messenger, it would seem, *does not want Jesus to encounter death*. The messenger speaks with a tone of authority. He has presumably examined the young girl or been with those who have certified her death. It is as if the messenger is tempting the Lord. Jesus will hear the temptation again, on the cross: "Save yourself and us" (Lk 23:39; see Mt 27:40), "[L]et him save himself" (Lk 23:35), and "Let the Messiah, the

King of Israel, come down from the cross now" (Mk 15:32, 36; see Mt 27:42). Jesus nonetheless moves forward and *ignores* the message to turn back. He calls on the official to have deeper faith: "Do not fear. Only believe, and she will be saved" (Lk 8:50; see Mk 5:36).

The world is full of messages that ask us to turn back from faith. There are some who seem to want death to be the final word. But something about death invites a deeper word, one that unlocks deeper faith. How often have you and I, like the Lord and Jarius, received the tragic word that someone has died? The moment of death is unlike any other. In that moment we hear those words of Jesus, "*only believe,*" in an entirely new way, as if for the first time.

Jesus arrives at the official's house and, as expected, he hears the din of the flute players and the loud weeping of the crowd. The funeral rites are underway and the wake has begun. Jesus announces that the child is not dead, but only sleeping. When Jesus says this, the crowd breaks from its commotion of grief to laugh at him. Luke even explains that the crowd laughs at the word of Jesus because *they know the girl is dead* (see Lk 8:53). The crowd has more faith in death than they do in Jesus. In this, the crowd is very similar to the messenger, perhaps worse. The messenger spoke as one who did not yet have faith; the crowd actually mocks Jesus. The word used for laughter in all three accounts is *katagelaō*, which means scornful derision. Notice, too, that the crowd's grief is as superficial as it is excessive. They move from wailing one moment to laughing the next. They would rather mock than mourn. This reveals that their grief is shallow, for it does not inhere in faith and love. Jesus has already entrusted his word to the official: "only believe." In the Old Testament, mourning that was unconnected to the hope held in store for us by God was forbidden (see Dt 14:1; Lv 19:28). In the accounts of Saint Matthew and Saint Mark, when the crowd begins to laugh, Jesus dismisses them from the house (see Mt 9:25; Mk 5:40). In Luke's account, in which they laugh at Jesus because they know she has died, the crowd remains. It is as if

Jesus wants them to see what he will do. Even in their obstinate disdain the Lord wants to evangelize them.

Jesus then takes the little girl by the hand, calls to her, and she arises. When Jesus heard Jairus' distress, his first action was to stand up, or to rise (*egeirō*), and follow him. When the little girl hears the life-giving word of Jesus, the Gospel tells us she likewise arose (*egeirō*). In a sense, she now imitates Jesus. Yet, there is a difference between this young girl's return to life and Jesus' resurrection on Easter Sunday. Jesus raises the little girl from the dead and brings her back to this life. Her resurrection is not the final resurrection. Rather, the Lord raising her from the dead is only a foreshadowing of his own resurrection on Easter. He then tells them to give her something to eat: the feast begins (see Jn 12:2).

A widowed mother burying her only son

> [Soon afterward] he went to a town called Nain, and his disciples and a large crowd went with him. As he approached the gate of the town, a man who had died was being carried out. He was his mother's only son, and she was a widow; and with her was a large crowd from the town. When the Lord saw her, he had compassion for her and said to her, "Do not weep." Then he came forward and touched the bier, and the bearers stood still. And he said, "Young man, I say to you, rise!" The dead man sat up and began to speak, and Jesus gave him to his mother. Fear seized all of them; and they glorified God, saying, "A great prophet has risen among us!" and "God has looked favorably on his people!" This word about him spread throughout Judea and all the surrounding country. (Lk 7:11–17)

As the Lord enters the city of Nain, a village in Galilee, with his disciples and a large crowd, he encounters a funeral procession approaching the city gate. In one sense the gate that the funeral procession approaches is the Lord *himself*. He is the gate to life (see Jn 10:9), the gate of the heavenly city, the narrow gate (see Mt 7:14; Lk

13:24). In some way every death passes by the Lord. And so, this day, a young man, the only son of his widowed mother, is being carried forth from the city. Like Jairus, the widowed mother is surrounded by a large crowd. Unlike in the healing of Jairus' daughter, Jesus has received no explicit invitation to this event.

The scene is strikingly similar to Good Friday. The body of the young man is being carried outside the city gate; on Good Friday Jesus will be crucified outside the city gate (see Heb 13:12). This young man is accompanied by his mother. The Blessed Mother will follow Jesus outside the city gate and be close to the body of the Lord after his death. Surely an inkling of his own mother is at work as Jesus meets this widow. When Jesus sees this sorrowful mother, he has compassion on her. Then he commands: "Do not weep" (Lk 7:13), just as he will tell the women he encounters on the road to Calvary not to weep for him, but for themselves and their children (see Lk 23:28). Jesus will weep over the city of Jerusalem (see Lk 19:41) and at the death of his friend Lazarus (see Jn 11:35).

The Gospel tells us that Jesus "came forward and touched the bier, and the bearers stood still" (Lk 7:14). He does not command the bearers to stop. Saint Cyril of Alexandria tells us that Jesus touched the bier so that we would be assured that his sacred flesh, his sacred humanity, is effective for our salvation.[2] Notice also that the bearers stop when he, the Son of the living God, touches the funeral bier. The Lord stops death in its tracks. Von Balthasar tells us that Jesus' physical act of touching the dead prefigures a very different touching, the touch the Risen Lord bestows through the sacraments on those who are living and dying.[3] In this passage the

---

2. See Saint Cyril of Alexandria, *Commentary on St. Luke, Homily 36* (New York: Studion Publishers, Inc, 1983), 155.

3. See Hans Urs von Balthasar, *Theodrama V: The Last Act*, 344.

word used for "stood still," *histēmi*, can refer to standing in the presence of a judge. Jesus is about to *judge* death.

The Greek word for "touch" used in the passage is *haptomai*. The root word for this expression means to set on fire or to set ablaze. Fire is a sign of the holiness of God. As with Moses and the burning bush, people are both drawn to fire and fear it. Jesus is the one who has come to set a fire on the earth (see Lk 12:49). The psalmist says "Our God comes and does not keep silence, before him is a devouring fire" (Ps 50:3). He is the one who answers with divine fire (see Gn 15:17; Dt 9:10; 1 Kgs 18:24; Is 6:6) that tests the heart of men (see 1 Cor 3:12–15). Fire has a twofold meaning in the Book of Revelation; it is a sign of God's presence and of his judgment (see Rev 1:14; 15:2; 19:12; 20:10 and 20:14ff.). He is the one who, judging death, will consume death and make the hearts of believers burn once again with love (see Lk 24:32).

And, at the city gate in Nain, the sentence is handed down: "Young man, I say to you, rise!" (Lk 7:14). The Greek word *egeirō* is again used here. We can see one final connection to Calvary in the account. Once the young man returns to life, Jesus gives him back to his mother. Jesus will make a similar act of entrustment as he gives the beloved disciple to his own mother at the foot of the cross (see Jn 19:27). Like the raising of Jairus' daughter, the resurrection of the son of the widow of Nain is a return to earthly life, not a resurrection to eternal life as Jesus experienced on Easter.

Lazarus

> Now a certain man was ill, Lazarus of Bethany, the village of Mary and her sister Martha. Mary was the one who anointed the Lord with perfume and wiped his feet with her hair; her brother Lazarus was ill. So the sisters sent a message to Jesus, "Lord, he whom you love is ill." But when Jesus heard it, he said, "This illness does not lead to death; rather it is for God's glory, so that the Son of God may be glorified through it." Accordingly, though

Jesus loved Martha and her sister and Lazarus, after having heard that Lazarus was ill, he stayed two days longer in the place where he was.

Then after this he said to the disciples, "Let us go to Judea again." . . . When Jesus arrived, he found that Lazarus had already been in the tomb four days. Now Bethany was near Jerusalem, some two miles away, and many of the Jews had come to Martha and Mary to console them about their brother. When Martha heard that Jesus was coming, she went and met him, while Mary stayed at home. Martha said to Jesus, "Lord, if you had been here, my brother would not have died. But even now I know that God will give you whatever you ask of him." Jesus said to her, "Your brother will rise again." Martha said to him, "I know that he will rise again in the resurrection on the last day." Jesus said to her, "I am the resurrection and the life. Those who believe in me, even though they die, will live, and everyone who lives and believes in me will never die. Do you believe this?" She said to him, "Yes, Lord, I believe that you are the Messiah, the Son of God, the one coming into the world."

When she had said this, she went back and called her sister Mary, and told her privately, "The Teacher is here and is calling for you." And when she heard it, she got up quickly and went to him. Now Jesus had not yet come to the village, but was still at the place where Martha had met him. The Jews who were with her in the house, consoling her, saw Mary get up quickly and go out. They followed her because they thought that she was going to the tomb to weep there. When Mary came where Jesus was and saw him, she knelt at his feet and said to him, "Lord, if you had been here, my brother would not have died." When Jesus saw her weeping, and the Jews who came with her also weeping, he was greatly disturbed in spirit and deeply moved. He said, "Where have you laid him?" They said to him, "Lord, come and see." Jesus began to weep. So the Jews said, "See how he loved him!" But some of them said, "Could not he who opened the eyes of the blind man have kept this man from dying?"

Then Jesus, again greatly disturbed, came to the tomb. It was a cave, and a stone was lying against it. Jesus said, "Take away the stone." Martha, the sister of the dead man, said to him, "Lord, already there is a stench because he has been dead four days." Jesus said to her, "Did I not tell you that if you believed, you would see the glory of God?" So they took away the stone. And Jesus looked upward and said, "Father, I thank you for having heard me. I knew that you always hear me, but I have said this for the sake of the crowd standing here, so that they may believe that you sent me." When he had said this, he cried with a loud voice, "Lazarus, come out!" The dead man came out, his hands and feet bound with strips of cloth, and his face wrapped in a cloth. Jesus said to them, "Unbind him, and let him go." (Jn 11:1–7, 17–44)

Jesus experiences death for the third time when his close friend Lazarus dies. Jesus had frequently visited Bethany, the home of Lazarus and his sisters Martha and Mary (see Mk 11:11; 14:3; Lk 10:38). The sisters now send a grim report to Jesus: the one "whom you love" is sick (Jn 11:3). The Greek word for love in this verse is *phileō*, which means to love like a brother or as a very close friend. Jesus tells his disciples that the sickness is not to end in death, but for the glory of God. The Gospel then tells us that "Jesus loved Martha and her sister and Lazarus." In this second instance the word used for love is not *phileō*, the word that Martha and Mary used, but *agapaō*. Of all the European languages, Greek has the most highly nuanced and developed manner of speaking of the nature of love.[4] Martha and Mary understand the love Jesus has for Lazarus as *phileō* love, the love of very close companions. But the Gospel tells us that the love with which Jesus loves Martha, Mary, and Lazarus surpasses *phileō*. He loves them with *agapaō* love, a selfless love that does not quit no matter what happens. Notice the distinction: Martha and

---

4. See Erasmo Leiva-Merikakis, *Love's Sacred Order: The Four Loves Revisited* (San Francisco: Ignatius Press, 2000), 49.

Mary experience the love of Jesus for Lazarus as companionship or friendship love. But the love that Jesus has for Lazarus, and for them, is actually a far deeper, self-sacrificing, unconditional love that is pure gift.

We, too, can misjudge love. In fact, in the case of Jesus, his love is divine charity: the very love by which God the Father loves Jesus (see Jn 10:17) and by which Jesus loves the Father (see Jn 14:31). *Agapaō* love has its source in the Holy Spirit. It is the love of the new commandment (see Jn 13:34); it is the love that Jesus promises to those who keep his commandments (see Jn 14:21). Already in the early verses of this passage, we are aware of a current that runs underneath all the activity: no matter how much we love God, he always loves us more, with a love that simply never quits.

In the context of this very love, and on hearing that Lazarus is sick, Jesus waits two days before going to him. We wonder why Jesus did not go immediately to see his friend who was ill. Saint Peter Chrysologos tells us that it was more important for Jesus to conquer death than to conquer the physical disease that afflicted Lazarus.[5] Saint Augustine points out that the sisters did not ask the Lord to come.[6] For Martha and Mary, it is enough for him to know about the illness. Something more is always at work in Jesus. Even his waiting is an invitation to love. By his loving delay, he is stretching the love of Martha and Mary from *phileō* to *agapaō*. The only way to grow love in such a manner is by faith and hope, which enlarges only through struggle. In the Lord's absence he is all the more present.

_____

5. See Saint Peter Chrysologos, *Sermon 63* as in E. Barnecut, ed. *Journey with the Fathers: Commentaries on the Sunday Gospels Year A* (New York: New City Press, 1992), Sermon 63:1–2; 44–45 PL 52:376.

6. See Saint Augustine, *Tractates on the Gospel of John* P. Schaff et al., eds. *A Select Library of the Nicene and Post-Nicene Fathers of the Christian Church* (Michigan: Eerdmans Press, 1994), 49.5; 1 7:272.

Without receiving another report, Jesus announces to the disciples that Lazarus has died. Jesus then says that he is glad he was not with Lazarus, so that the disciples may believe. Adrienne von Speyr points out that Lazarus' death thus takes on the character of a promise and of a beginning.[7] By the time Jesus arrives, Lazarus has already been in the tomb four days. Martha meets the Lord and says, "Lord, if you had been here, my brother would not have died. But even now I know that God will give you whatever you ask of him" (Jn 11:21–22). Jesus proclaims that Lazarus will rise again. Martha responds, "I know that he will rise again" on the last day. The Greek word for "know" is *eidō*, which means to see with the senses or to perceive as a fact. Martha has not yet responded with faith, but with knowledge. Von Balthasar points out that the Lord counters Martha sharply and proclaims: "I am the resurrection and the life. Those who believe in me, even though they die, will live, and everyone who lives and believes in me will never die. Do you believe this?" (Lk 11:25–26).[8] "Jesus links faith in the resurrection to his own person" (*CCC* 994). When Martha states her knowledge, Jesus asks for faith. Martha responds, "Yes, Lord, I believe that you are the Messiah, the Son of God, the one coming into the world" (Jn 11:27). Her faith is growing.

As with the synagogue official, Jesus summons *living* faith. Notice that after their conversation about faith, the very next thing Martha does is to go and *call* her sister Mary: "The Teacher is here and is calling for you" (Jn 11:28). The text tells us that Martha called her sister "privately" or "secretly." The Greek word for "secretly" is *lathra*, which can also mean "to be hidden away." This word describes

---

7. See Adrienne von Speyr, *John: The Discourses of Controversy, Meditations on John 6–12* (San Francisco: Ignatius Press, 1993), 309.

8. See Hans Urs von Balthasar, *Theodrama V*, 24.

the action of Jesus himself when he hid away and wanted no one to know about his movements (see Mk 7:24). In a sense the word refers to Mary herself, the contemplative who is hidden in the Lord. She imitates the very action of Jesus. Even more, nowhere does the passage state that Jesus has explicitly asked for Mary. At a deeper level, when Jesus asks for faith, Martha's further response is to summon her sister, the contemplative. When Jesus asks us for faith, he is leading us to disappear into contemplation, into the hidden life. As soon as Mary hears that Jesus is calling her, she rises quickly and goes to Jesus. The word for "rises" is the "resurrection" word we have encountered several times already, *egeirō*. Notice also that the crowd follows Mary to Jesus. They did not follow Martha when she went to the Lord, but they do follow Mary, the contemplative. It seems as if the first message Martha and Mary sent to Jesus, "He whom you love is ill," was a prayer of petition that has become a prayer of contemplation.

As she comes to Jesus, Mary falls at his feet—where she had once sat (see Lk 10:39; Jn 12:3). She shows reverence for Jesus just as Jairus, the synagogue official, had given him homage. Notice Mary repeats the words Martha had spoken only a few verses earlier: "Lord, if you had been here, my brother would not have died" (Jn 11:32). When Jesus sees her faith, when he sees the contemplative and those with her weeping, he groans in his spirit (*embrimaomai pneuma*) and is troubled (*kai tarassō heautou*). Belief elicits something further from the very depths of the Lord. And he says, "Where have you laid him?" (Jn 11:34). The Lord knew of the death of Lazarus long before arriving; he would know very well where they have laid him. He asks the people to lead him and, by this question, he is now bonded to all mourners of every time and space. His question is a summons to humanity to walk with him to the place of cruel fate and utmost fear: the tomb. As he approaches the burial place, Jesus is again troubled in spirit, and he commands them to

"Take away the stone" (Jn 11:39). Although Jesus could have dramatically moved the stone himself, he summons others to do so. One day he will summon their faith to move mountains, but now, only this stone (see Mt 17:20).

They must now touch what they fear. The Lord bypasses no distress and leaves no suffering behind. It is now even clearer that Jesus is walking with them, step by treacherous step, to the place they and we fear the most: the dark and still interior of the tomb. Martha protests, "Lord, already there is a stench because he has been dead four days" (Jn 11:39). Her faith is wavering, but even her doubt serves the great miracle he is about to work. Martha attests beyond doubt to the irrefutable fact of Lazarus' physical death. The action about to take place is no mere resuscitation from a coma.

Jesus prays: "Father, I thank you for having heard me. I knew that you always hear me, but I have said this for the sake of the crowd standing here, so that they may believe that you sent me" (Jn 11:41–42). The miracle about to take place emerges from the heart of Jesus' communion with his Father. Notice that in his prayer Jesus speaks to his Father not about Lazarus, but about *the crowd*. As much as he will raise Lazarus, he endeavors to raise up faith in the heart of the crowd. He asks that they may believe, for as he has told Martha, ". . . if you believed, you would see the glory of God" (Jn 11:40).

Jesus then calls out in a loud voice, "Lazarus, come out" (Lk 11:43). The details preceding this miracle are quite different from those of the raising of Jairus' daughter and the widow of Nain. In the raising of Lazarus, we are not told that the Lord touches him. Two things are important here. First, the voice of the Lord is all-sufficient to summon life. The miracle prefigures the victorious death and resurrection of Jesus, by which the Lord will bestow the gift of his divine life on the world. The Creator summons his creation. Second, the touch is bestowed not by the Lord, but by those whom he is summoning to a living and deep faith: "Take away the stone" (Jn

11:39), and, "Unbind him, and let him go" (Jn 11:44). Notice also that when Jesus tells Jairus' daughter to rise, he calls her "Little girl" (Mk 5:41) or "child" (Lk 8:54). Here, too, he calls Lazarus by name (see Jn 11:43). The Fathers of the Church tell us that the word of life that abides in the Son of the living God is so powerful that if the Lord had not specified Lazarus to "come forth," every corpse in the cemetery would have risen.[9]

Lazarus comes out of the tomb still bound by the burial clothes, unable to free himself. This illustrates the difference between the resurrection of Lazarus, who rises to a restored earthly life, and that of Jesus, who rises to eternal life. With the command, "Unbind him, and let him go" (Jn 11:44), Jesus once again summons the crowd to allow their faith to replace their fears.

A sign and pledge

We have every reason to believe Jesus experienced the death of many people. In due course, his friends, neighbors, and even relatives passed away. In fact, Jesus must have experienced great pain on learning of the death of his cousin, Saint John the Baptist (see Mt 14:12). Even though he loved them dearly, the Lord did not raise all those who passed away during his public ministry. The miracles Jesus performed—the raising of Jairus' daughter, of the son of the widow of Nain, and of Lazarus—are not only wonders meant to prove the Lord's divinity. They are far more. During his public ministry, Jesus miraculously restores the dead to mortal life as a sign and pledge that he will raise the faithful departed on the last day, not to return them to this earthly life, but as a share in his own divine life

9. See Maximinus *Sermon 14* as in *Corpus Christianorum,* Series Latina (Belgium: Turnhout, 1953), 87:28.

(see *CCC* 994). These mighty deeds point to the ultimate victory of Jesus over sin and death. They point to *the* mighty deed of Christ in his cross and resurrection by which "[t]he innocent Jesus, out of pure love, entered into solidarity with the guilty and thus transformed their situation from within."[10] In the wondrous plan of God, death is overcome not from without, but from *within*.[11] In this we find the great testimony to his divinity.

---

10. Saint John Paul II, *Jesus, Son and Savior*, 445.
11. See Hans Urs von Balthasar, *Theodrama IV*, 493, 495.

CHAPTER NINE

The Cross of Jesus: Death Overcome from Within

First words are very important. In the Book of Genesis, God's very first words to man are, "You are free . . ." (Gn 2:16 NABRE). From the very beginning, Adam was entrusted with his own freedom, and he freely chose to reject God and sin. Adam is the representative of the entire human race. Saint Paul therefore says of Adam's sin: "Sin came into the world through one man, and death came through sin . . ." (Rom 5:12). Death entered the world because Adam freely decided to reject God, his Creator. Because Adam sinned freely, and because each personal sin we commit is a free choice, God does not resolve sin and death with random wave of his hand so as to arbitrarily undo our free sinful choice. Why doesn't he? Because God is not a remote, omnipotent scorekeeper who is simply out to penalize us one moment and then casually void our free choice in the next, thereby undoing the wages of sin, which is death. Sin is not merely a "stepping out of bounds." Love, to really be love, must be freely given and received. And sin is a free choice to refuse God's love. God takes human sin seriously because God takes love seriously. *God takes us and our freedom seriously*—our choice to either love him or to freely disobey and deliberately reject him. So God does not indiscriminately bypass or minimize human sin. "God is love" (1 Jn 4:8, 16). As Saint John Paul II taught, in the mystery of redemption, mercy is an essential dimension of love. Mercy is the second name of love.[1] In mercy, God does something infinitely more loving than to casually dismiss man's fault. Mercy does not minimize sin, or it would be no more than God pretending that sin had never happened. Mercy is love doing more, and God always does more: "For God so loved the world that he gave his only Son" (Jn 3:16). Love does not simply void or defy true freedom, otherwise it is not love, but *autonomy*. God always remains a God of love. Love does not pretend or deny even the hardest of realities, but love faces reality. For God's plan to be *true* to God and to us, God must now respond *completely* to the deliberate evil that human sin has done.

Now the degree of an offense is measured by the dignity of the one offended. Since God's dignity is infinite, Adam and Eve's *offense* against him was infinite. Therefore, the satisfaction for sin must be infinite. Yet the infinite remedy for the offense must *truly arise from the man, the one who bears the burden of the offense*. How could man's finite nature offer an infinite remedy? The astounding truth is that God, from the depths of his infinite love, stepped onto the world stage and took on our flesh—truly becoming man without ceasing to be God—in order to *save* man. God sent his eternal Son to take our place, to *undergo* death and so to save us from death and to restore our unity with God. "God has made his own the tragic

---

1. See Saint John Paul II, *Dives in misericordia*, no. 7.

situation of human existence."[2] The Fathers of the Church quote one verse from the New Testament more than any other to explain why Christ had to die: "Since, therefore, the children share flesh and blood, he himself [Jesus] likewise shared the same things, so that through death he might destroy the one who has the power of death, that is, the devil, and free those who all their lives were held in slavery by the fear of death" (Heb 2:14–15).[3]

Earlier I described the unexpectedness of seeing a crucifix in the coffin at the first wake service I attended. We often see the crucifix. It is prominently displayed in every Catholic church either above or near the altar. The crucifix is lifted high and carried in procession at the beginning and end of Mass. Many people wear a small crucifix on a chain around their neck. It is part of the rosary beads we carry. Sometimes we see a dramatic painting of the crucifixion, or find it depicted on a holy card. The custom of carrying a small crucifix in our pocket reminds us of the saving action of Christ even when we routinely reach for coins or car keys. When we see the crucifix, we are plunged into the science of salvation even at the most ordinary moments.

The crucifix we see in church, wear as jewelry, or carry in our pocket is meant to *do* something. We see it so often that we can forget its mysteries are infinite. It always has more to teach us. It reminds us that at the center of our faith is the crucifixion of the Son of God for us. Sometimes we can compartmentalize our faith, perhaps identifying it with one or two specific aspects that we happen to be involved with. For example, we can identify our faith with

---

2. Hans Urs von Balthasar, *Theodrama II*, 54.

3. Louis Bouyer, *The Spirituality of the New Testament and the Fathers* (New York: Desclée Company, 1960), 144.

action: we perform a corporal work of mercy by feeding the hungry and welcoming the stranger. Or perhaps we identify our faith with private devotional practices. We may even identify our faith with volunteering at our parish or with the friends we meet through our prayer group. These are all very important and good. Yet they are all rooted in something deeper..

Faith is not first about what we *do*, but about *Who* we know: Jesus Christ. Through faith we have a personal and living relationship with Jesus Christ in and through the Church. And when we know Christ, we first know him crucified and risen. All of Jesus' beautiful sayings in Scripture, his prayerful moments, his parables, his miracles, and his teachings *lead to* and *flow from* his cross and resurrection. In fact, unless they are illuminated by his suffering, death, and resurrection—the rest remain somehow incomplete for us. The height and the depth of knowing Jesus is to know him in his passion, death, and resurrection.

Earlier we discovered the important clue that death entered the world through Satan's envy. In his pride, Satan's envy arose because he foresaw that the Son of God would bypass angelic nature to assume human nature. Out of hatred for God, the devil seeks to destroy God's plan. The diabolical plot proceeds. If the devil destroys human beings, he destroys human nature. If he destroys human nature, he destroys God's plan to send his only Son to assume human nature in the mystery of the Incarnation. The devil wielded the weapon of sin to destroy human beings, because the consequence of sin is death. If by sin the human race brings death upon itself, the Son of God could not assume human nature, or so the devil thought. He thought our death was his future. Death is always his only solution.

But God is a God of life. Immediately after human sin, God promises in the *Protoevangelium* to send his only Son to save us from sin and death. When the Son of God assumed human nature and took flesh at the Incarnation, the devil turned again to his weapon: death. He sought to kill the Lord in the slaughter of the Holy Innocents (see Mt 2:16–18); by means of the temptations: "throw yourself down" (Mt 4:6); and by the conspiracy of the various crowds (see Mt 12:14; Mk 3:6; Lk 4:29, 22:1–6; Jn 11:45ff.). The innocent Son of God is on a collision course with the sin of the world. In a fallen world, goodness does not have to go far to find itself in the battle with evil. In his pride and envy, the devil thinks that if he can kill Jesus, God in the flesh, then he will finally win; he will take the place of God.

Pride blinds. The same prideful darkness that led Satan to oppose the plan of God leads him to attack the Son of God. And so, the sacred passion of our Lord begins (see Mt 26:36ff.; Mk 15ff.; Lk 22:47ff.; Jn 18ff.). From the agony in the Garden, to the betrayal by Judas and throughout the trial, the Lord suffers. His torment increases with the scourging, the condemnation to death, the mockery and the crowning with thorns, the carrying of the cross and the crucifixion. On Good Friday Satan thought he was winning. He thought the death of the Son of God would be the end, but Satan was wrong. Pride cannot see love, and each moment of the plan of redemption takes place on the initiative of absolute divine love: "No one has greater love than this, to lay down one's life for one's friends" (Jn 15:13).

The love of the Lord is infinite: "He loved them to the end" (Jn 13:1). Saint John further emphasizes, "We know love by this, that he laid down his life for us" (1 Jn 3:16). He gave his life as "a ransom for many" (Mk 10:45; see Mt 20:28; 1 Tim 2:5–6). The culmination of the divine plan of love takes place as the Son of God gives himself entirely for the salvation of the world. In his infinite, redeeming love, the sinless Son loaded onto himself every human sin throughout history. The prophet Isaiah foretold it long ago: "He shall bear their iniquities" (Is 53:11, 4). Because Jesus is *true man* he can take on *all human* sin, and because he is *true God* he is able to offer himself as an *infinite* sacrifice. Christ "taste[d] death for everyone" (Heb 2:9). Saint Paul takes us to the very heart of the mystery: "For the love of Christ urges us on, because we are convinced that one has died for all; therefore all have died. And he died for all, so that those who live might live no longer for themselves, but for him who died and was raised for them" (2 Cor 5:14–15). Saint Pope John Paul II affirms: "He who 'knew no sin'—the Son, consubstantial with the Father—took upon himself the terrible burden of the sin of all humanity, in order to obtain our justification and sanctification."[4]

The mystery of the cross is a mystery of love. It is not an instance of the Father God taking bloodthirsty and violent vengeance on his own Son for the sin of the human race. Rather, the unspeakable and awful sufferings of the guiltless Son of God on the cross display the absolute horror of the world's sin. The sacrifice by which the Son atones for human sin is not designed to placate God as if, enraged at this sin, he has crossed his arms in some distant heaven and turned his back until a precise measure of revenge is exacted. *It is quite the opposite.* The Son of God is *not* distant; he is *here*, on Calvary: "My Father is still working, and I also am working" (Jn 5:17). In response to human sin, the Father *bends close* and the Spirit *hovers* above the precise center of the salvific mission of the Son on the cross to free us from sin. *We are the ones who have crossed our arms and turned our backs.* Our hardened hearts cannot be convinced by anything less than the sacrifice offered upon the cross by the Son of God himself.

As we ponder the reality of the cross, its mystery stands out all the more: sin is completely distant from God and his absolute love. Abiding in the most profound unity with the Father and the Holy

---

4. Saint John Paul II, *Jesus, Son and Savior*, 427.

Spirit, the Son accepts the mission from the Father to bear all that is distant from God, namely, to bear the sin of the entire world: "He is the atoning sacrifice for our sins, and not for ours only but also for the sins of the whole world" (1 Jn 2:2; see 3:5; 4:10; Rom 3:25). This is not an automatic or merely ceremonial moment. Imagine its startling proportions. In the obedient charity of self-surrendering love, the Son goes to the utterly unimaginable depths of divine love and takes *on himself* the entire weight of all that is foreign and removed from God's pure, divine love. He absorbs all the full, terrible weight of the alienation and forsakenness of every sin throughout human history and suffers an unspeakable collision.[5] Even more wondrously, in taking sin on himself, the Son does not experience reprobation as if he himself had sinned.[6] And yet, Christ endures the brutal fury of every human suffering on the cross.[7] He is the completely innocent Victim who takes on the full burden of the world's sin: "He himself bore our sins in his body on the cross, so that, free from sins, we might live for righteousness; by his wounds you have been healed" (1 Pet 2:24–25). The Father "did not withhold his own Son, but gave him up for all of us" (Rom 8:32; see 1 Cor 15:3; Heb 9:26).

The devil, through those standing near the cross, tempts the Son one final time: "If you are the Son of God, come down from the cross" (Mt 27:40). This challenge mimics the first temptation put to the human race: "You will not die!" (Gn 3:4). And so, the Son of God suffers as the abysmal weight of all the temptations and sins of all human history. It all falls totally upon Christ. And this is

_____

5. See Hans Urs von Balthasar, *The Glory of the Lord VII*, 210.
6. See *CCC* 603; see also Balthasar, *Theodrama IV*, 336.
7. See *STh* IIIa, q 46, a 5–7.

precisely why: "For in him every one of God's promises is a 'Yes'" (2 Cor 1:20), and his "yes" to the Father, in the Holy Spirit, is a generous "yes" without measure that stretches beyond all comparison.[8] He suffers and dies for all people everywhere and without exception. With each breath as he hung on the cross, Jesus drew the entire world to himself. This living breath of love draws us beyond death. The heart of the cross is love. And mercy is the unfathomable moment that the cross "dissolves punishment in love."[9]

Our Lord's cry from the cross

As we listen closely we hear the great drama of God's triune love breaking through. The Son surrenders himself in such untold and absolute love for the Father in the Holy Spirit that he cries out, "My God, my God, why have you forsaken me?" (Mt 27:46; see Mk 15:34; Ps 22). He experiences the abandonment by God.[10] This is a great mystery.

> Jesus had the clear vision of God and the certainty of his union with the Father dominant in his mind. But in the sphere bordering on the senses . . . Jesus' human soul was regarded as a wasteland. He no longer felt the presence of the Father, but he underwent the tragic experience of the most complete desolation.[11]

Entire, unreserved love emerges from the heart of God. The Son has taken upon himself the full weight of all human sin, yet he

---

8. See Hans Urs von Balthasar, *Theodrama III*, 113 and 115; see also *The Glory of the Lord VII*, 284.

9. See Hans Urs von Balthasar, *Theologic III: The Spirit of Truth*, 363.

10. See Saint John Paul II, *Jesus, Son and Savior*, 471.

11. Ibid., 472; see *STh* IIIa, q 46, a 8.

always remains within the inexhaustible, loving, superabundant communion with the Father, in the Holy Spirit.[12] In him the full depths of the self-giving, eternal love of God collide head-on with the abysmal self-taking of human sin. The complete, terrifying reality of sin is exposed, and it all converges at once upon the Son. On Good Friday, "the abyss of the unfathomable love has entered the abyss of the meaningless hatred and hidden itself there."[13] The result is that the Crucified, in the moment of his ultimate suffering, utters a loud cry. Saint Luke tells us: "Then Jesus, crying with a loud voice, said, 'Father, into your hands I commend my spirit.' Having said this, he breathed his last" (Lk 23:46; see Mt 27:50, Mk 15:37). Saint John says, "[H]e gave up his spirit" (Jn 19:30). In the Lord's cry from the cross, God's judgment is now fully pronounced once and for all on human sin.[14] The Son's cry is beyond words.[15] Eternal love resounds in a cry of unequaled powerlessness. The Son is "The One who conquers by total self-surrender."[16] Pope Benedict XVI tells us that Jesus "has truly gone right to the end, to the very limit and even beyond that limit. He has accomplished the utter fullness of love—he has given himself."[17] And in this unfathomable moment the Son of God on the cross pours himself out even further in immeasurable love. In his death he destroys sin and confers on us, in and through the Church, a share in his own divinity. He reveals the full magnitude of the verse from the Song of Songs: "Love is strong

---

12. *CCC* 606; Hans Urs von Balthasar, *Theodrama V: The Last Act*, 68.

13. Hans Urs von Balthasar, *The Glory of the Lord VII*, 210.

14. See Hans Urs von Balthasar, *Theodrama V*, 261–262.

15. See Hans Urs Balthasar, *The Glory of the Lord VII*, 210.

16. Hans Urs von Balthasar, *Theodrama II*, 161.

17. Pope Benedict XVI, *Jesus of Nazareth Part II*, 223; see also Hans Urs von Balthasar, *Theologic III: The Spirit of Truth*, 300.

as death" (8:6). This is the great sacrifice on the part of the Son, from which he creates the new intimacy of infinite love for us based on his own intimacy with the Father in the Holy Spirit. "Now the ruler of this world will be driven out" (Jn 12:31).

The Lord truly died; he experienced an end to his earthly human existence. The Son's death is the "most lonely" of all deaths.[18] Yet at the moment when the Son "breathed his last," something happened: he "handed over the spirit" both to the Father and to the world.[19] In the cross is revealed the mysterious, unfathomable, and utterly complete inner depths of the abiding humble love existing between the Father and the Son in the Holy Spirit. Saint Thomas tells us that the Lord's death on the tree of the cross atoned for the sin of Adam who reached out disobediently to the forbidden tree: "All that Adam lost, Christ found upon the cross."[20]

The Son's death is an act of obedience without limits. His victorious act on the cross brings an endless measure of Trinitarian self-giving love into the most dense and absolutely dark moment of all human history. Saint Pope John Paul II points out that "the whole Trinity was present in his passion."[21] The Father surrenders his only begotten Son: "he . . . did not withhold his own Son" (Rom 8:32). The Holy Spirit is the Person-Love who *"comes down, in a certain sense, into the very heart of the sacrifice* which is offered on the cross. . . . He consumes this sacrifice with the fire of the love that unites the Son with the Father in the Trinitarian communion."[22]

18. Hans Urs von Balthasar, *Theodrama IV*, 133, 336.

19. See Hans Urs von Balthasar, *Theologic III: The Spirit of Truth*, 294.

20. *Summa Theologiae* IIIa q 46, a 4.

21. Saint John Paul II, *The Trinity's Embrace: God's Saving Plan* (Boston: Pauline Books & Media, 2002), 69.

22. Saint John Paul II, *Dominum et vivificantem*, no. 41.

The Holy Spirit draws us into the grace-filled, eternal newness of unsurpassable and absolute self-giving love.[23] "Through the Holy Spirit, Jesus in his paschal mystery communicates to us in its fullness the 'eternal life' that flows from the Father."[24] Death is forever changed. The penalty is permanently transformed from a dead end into a new beginning. In his powerlessness on the cross, the Son turns the course of history into eternity. The eternal Son of God becomes man so that he may pay the debt for the sin of man. Yet, as he enters into solidarity with us and takes our place so as to satisfy the infinite debt of sin, the Son, in that same solidarity, draws us into his infinitude: "The Word became flesh to make us *'partakers of the divine nature'*" (2 Pet 1:4).

The crucifix in our churches or worn about the neck is no mere emblem, fancy artwork, or piece of jewelry. It is the sacred symbol of the victorious Christ. Each time we see it, the crucifix reminds us of and leads us deeper into the mystery of Christ's saving death and the promise of resurrection. The words of the psalmist resound: "One generation shall laud your works to another, and shall declare your mighty acts. On the glorious splendor of your majesty, and on your wondrous works, I will meditate . . . and I will declare your greatness" (Ps 145:4–6). In the sacrament of Baptism, we *enter into* this moment of Christ's victory in his death and resurrection. That is why a crucifix is placed on the top of coffins at funeral masses. Christ had conquered death and the man or woman who had died had been baptized into Christ's death, and thus they share in Christ's resurrection. Likewise, that person had also received the Holy Eucharist, the

---

23. See Hans Urs von Balthasar, *Theodrama V: The Last Act*, 82.
24. Saint John Paul II, *The Trinity's Embrace*, 137.

sacrament of Christ's real presence by which the Lord shares with us his gift of love offered on the cross. In faith, everyone who sees the crucifix on the coffin at the celebration of Holy Mass at a funeral is unfailingly called to an even deeper trust in that life-giving promise given from the cross.

Because the Son of God, a divine Person, experienced death in his human nature, the death of every believer is forever changed and filled with new meaning. The Son bows his head in the direction of the earth, and in this inscrutable moment he forever offers the hidden gift of the Holy Spirit in a completely new way. The Spirit hovered over the womb of the Virgin Mary to bring the Son into the world. The Son now hovers over the world and bestows the Spirit.[25] Since the Son of God has united himself with every person, every Christian death now has the capacity to access the gift of the Holy Spirit.

The wound in Our Lord's side

Saint John tells us that shortly after Jesus' death, a soldier thrusts a spear into the side of his body as it hangs upon the cross. Immediately blood and water flow forth (see Jn 19:34). The spear witnesses to the Lord's total self-gift. Paul Claudel tells us that the spear penetrated further than Christ's heart: the spear opened God and found its way into the very heart of the Trinitarian love.[26] The sacrifice is immediately fruitful.[27] The infinite charity of the Lord releases the gifts of the Eucharist and Baptism. Through the

25. See Hans Urs von Balthasar, *Theologic III: The Spirit of Truth*, 175.

26. See Paul Claudel, *I Believe in God: A Meditation on the Apostles' Creed* (San Francisco: Ignatius Press, 2002), 132.

27. See Saint John Paul II, *Jesus, Son and Savior*, 481.

shedding of his most precious blood, the Son ransoms the sinner (see 1 Jn 1:7). On the cross, the Son accomplishes the supreme action of infinite love: he is obedient unto death. Saint Paul calls our attention to the perfect self-emptying of the Son:

> who, though he was in the form of God,
>   did not regard equality with God
>   as something to be exploited,
> but emptied himself,
>   taking the form of a slave,
>   being born in human likeness.
> And being found in human form,
>   he humbled himself
>   and became obedient to the point of death—
> even death on a cross. (Phil 2:6–8)

The Son's self-emptying obedience expresses the true face of absolute love: humility (see 2 Tim 1:10; Heb 2:14). In pouring himself out upon the cross, he does what he has been doing for all eternity. The Son pours himself out in love eternally to the Father in the Holy Spirit. Every action of the Son in time reflects his eternal posture before the Father. The Son pours himself out when he assumes human nature in the womb of the Virgin Mary; he pours himself out when he is born in a stable, when he has nowhere to lay his head, when he is falsely accused, mocked, and spat upon by the very creature he has created, and when he empties himself in his sacred passion. And he does all of this out of love. So dramatic is the self-emptying of the Son that even Pilate catches a glimpse of light when he points to the Lord in the extreme humility of his suffering and proclaims: "*Ecce Homo!* Behold, the man!" (Jn 19:5 NABRE). The eternal Son's response to the evil sin's self-taking is to pour himself out all the more in the perfect sacrifice of utter self-giving love.

The contours of God's plan become clear: where Adam faltered, Jesus opens a new way: "For just as by the one man's disobedience the many were made sinners, so by the one man's obedience the many will be made righteous" (Rom 5:19). This is the utterly astonishing mission of the Son: He fills not only life, but also *suffering and death* with a new and unimaginable meaning: "As the Word, a divine Person, he confers an infinite value on his suffering and death. . . ."[28] Whereas Adam chose the finite, Christ chooses the infinite. The all-sufficient, grace-filled merit of the Son's perfect, unique, and definitive sacrifice brings redemption and complete atonement for all sin (*CCC* 613–617). There is no other means of salvation. Jesus is the one mediator between God and man (see 1 Tim 2:5–6). "There is salvation in no one else, for there is no other name under heaven given among mortals by which we must be saved" (Acts 4:12; see Lk 1:31; Mt 1:21; *CCC* 618).

On the cross, Christ is the wondrous warrior who freed the human race with his wounds. Death becomes life. Decay becomes immortality.[29] Shame becomes glory. For this reason Theodore the Studite proclaims that the cross, "is wholly beautiful to behold and good to taste."[30] Death is slain; Adam is restored to life. The cross is the priceless treasure at the center of our lives. His victory does not remain simply a past event. The cross of Jesus not only destroys sin, but it also initiates the believer into the life of the Triune God. Not only are we forgiven, the price paid in full, but we are also now invited to participate in the grace-filled, all-sufficient merit of Jesus Christ, secured on the cross, flowing to us through the sacraments, especially the Eucharist. The Lord institutes the Holy Eucharist at the Last Supper on Holy Thursday

---

28. Saint John Paul II, *Jesus: Son and Savior*, 439.

29. Auer, Ratzinger, *Eschatology: Death and Eternal Life*, 193.

30. Theodore the Studite, *Oratio in Adorationem Crucis*: PG 99, 691–694; 698–699.

evening, the night before he died. In that Supper he anticipates the action of the cross on Good Friday. He mandates the apostles to perpetuate the celebration of the Holy Eucharist as the New Covenant for the sanctification of the world. The sacraments draw the believer into the drama of salvation so that, by sharing in the saving death of Christ, the believer passes from death to life even now (see Jn 5:24).

Christ's descent among the dead

The Lord died. He was laid in the tomb. Even the Lord's tomb plays a role in the mystery. The very stones shout out the mystery as the tomb receives the body of the Lord (see Lk 19:40). The tomb fittingly testifies in at least three ways. First, he who was born of the Virgin is laid to rest in a new tomb in which no one had been buried. Second, he who was born in the poverty of a stable and had nowhere to lay his head is marked by poverty even in death. The One who commanded us to clothe the naked is now clothed by Joseph of Arimathea. Third, the Lord, who died for the salvation of others is buried in a stranger's grave. Saint Thomas and Saint Augustine both comment on how fitting that is.[31] Even the tomb is configured to the mystery that unfolds in its secret depths.

Between his death on the cross and his resurrection, the Lord truly experienced the separation of his soul from his body.[32] His soul was glorified in God in the fullness of the beatific vision, but his body was placed in the tomb as a corpse.[33] Yet, Christ's Godhead was not,

---

31. See *STh* IIIa, q 51, a 2 and Saint Augustine, *Sermon* 248.
32. See *CCC* 624; see also Saint John Paul II, *Jesus, Son and Savior*, 485.
33. See Saint John Paul II, *Jesus, Son and Savior*, 485.

for that reason, separated from his body when he died.[34] The divine person of Christ remains united to his soul and to his body even when these are separated from one another in death (*CCC* 650). The Son is present in heaven and he is present among the dead. The psalmist expresses this mystery with simplicity, "If I ascend to heaven, you are there; if I make my bed in Sheol, you are there" (Ps 139:8).

Sheol is translated as *Hades* in Greek. It is the realm of the netherworld.[35] Entering the tomb becomes a symbol of entry to the region of the dead. *Sheol* comes about because of sin. The psalmist describes death as a descent into the Pit (see Ps 18:5–6; 30:10), to the region incompatible with fullness of life. More starkly, those in *Sheol* are cut off from God: "For in death there is no remembrance of you; in Sheol who can give you praise?" (Ps 6:5), and: "The dead do not praise the LORD, nor do any that go down into silence" (Ps 115:17). The psalmist describes the grave as a state of utter deprivation and abandonment (see Ps 13:4; 49:15). For this reason, *Sheol* is a region of shadowy darkness and gloom (see Ps 88:7, 13; Ez 28:8; 31:14), "the land of gloom and chaos, where light is like darkness" (Job 10:22). But *Sheol* is not the hell of eternal damnation; it is the "hell" of the Fathers, the dwelling of all those, good and evil, who have died since the time of Adam, and await the Savior, imprisoned until the resurrection of Christ (see Acts 3:15; Rom 8:11; 1 Cor 15:20; Heb 13:20). Jesus does not deliver the damned from *Sheol*. He descends to free the just who are detained there have been deprived of the vision of God (*CCC* 633).

---

34. See *STh* IIIa, q 50, a 2–3; q 52, a 3.
35. See Xavier Léon Dufour, *Resurrection and the Message of Easter*, trans. R. N. Wilson (New York: Holt, 1974), 11; see also *CCC* 633.

The time the Lord spends in the tomb takes us into the mystery of his descent into hell, the mystery of Holy Saturday. Saint Paul tells us that Jesus "descended into the lower parts of the earth" (Eph 4:9). He did so in his human soul united to his divine Person (*CCC* 636). By his descent among the dead, the Son continues his saving mission. Saint Peter explains, "[T]he gospel was proclaimed even to the dead" (1 Pet 4:6). This is so that "the dead will hear the voice of the Son of God, and those who hear will live" (Jn 5:25; see Mt 12:40 and Rom 10:7) as he "deliver[s] their soul[s] from death" (Ps 33:19). During his speech on Pentecost, Saint Peter reminds his listeners of the words of King David, "I saw the Lord always before me, for he is at my right hand so that I will not be shaken; therefore my heart was glad, and my tongue rejoiced; moreover my flesh will live in hope. For you will not abandon my soul to Hades, or let your Holy One experience corruption" (Acts 2:25–27; see Ps 16:8–11). Saint Peter emphasized that God had sworn an oath to David, that he would not abandon him to the netherworld. The descent into hell is the fulfillment of God's undying faithfulness: "But God will ransom my soul from the power of Sheol, for he will receive me" (Ps 49:15), and he "snatched them from the grave" (Ps 107:20 NABRE).

By his descent among the dead, the Son takes on himself the complete weight of the tomb. The Son has found his way not only into the maze of life, but also into the maze of death. By the entrance of Christ into the mystery of his descent among the dead, even *Sheol* is *transformed*, making the immeasurable victory of Christ shine forth all the more. Even here, the promise of God is not exhausted or extinguished, and his majesty and glory shine forth all the more. Just as God laid bare the depths of the Red Sea when he saved the Israelites from slavery in Egypt, so too, his Son has laid bare the depths of the netherworld. The mystery of the Son's descent among the dead is *a mystery of salvation* and portrays, in vivid fashion, Jesus Christ's complete solidarity with the human race. By dying, the Son has truly united himself to the death of every person.[36] In love the Son pours himself out as he descends to the region of alienation and loneliness, seeking to deliver the believer from slavery to sin and death. He goes to rescue the just ones who are imprisoned there: "he brings up from the great abyss" (Tob 13:2) in an unmistakable sign of his primordial power over the forces of death.[37] The Son's descent into *Sheol* is the continuation of his unfathomable love, a love that continually seeks to pour itself out and *unite* itself to man. He "shatters the doors of bronze" (Ps 107:16) asunder and, in his invincible love, he cleanses the just so that they may be separated from him no longer.

The risen Lord holds the "keys of death and Hades" (Rev 1:18). He, the inexhaustible and superabundant Source of new life, has "gone to look for Adam so that he might fulfill man's salvation (see Jn 19:30)."[38] The Good Shepherd has gone to the farthest reaches to search out and deliver all of the just since Adam, who have been banished to *Sheol* as a consequence of sin. "For you have power over life and death; you lead mortals down to the gates of Hades and back again" (Wis 16:13). Von Balthasar poetically writes that the cross is erected at the end of hell.[39] Christ has conquered *Sheol* so that he might fill the emptiness of death with meaning and life.[40] By his death and descent among

---

36. See *STh* IIIa, q 50, a 4.

37. See Hans Urs von Balthasar, *The Glory of the Lord VI: The Old Covenant*, 77.

38. See *CCC* 624, 635; see also, Ancient Homily for Holy Saturday: PG 43, 44. A 452C: LH, Holy Saturday, OR.

39. See Hans Urs von Balthasar, *Theodrama IV*, 495.

40. See *The Church's Confession of Faith*, 163.

the dead, Christ has extended the plan of redemption to all generations of all distant times and places.

Reverence for the body of the deceased

The sacrament of Baptism unites the Christian with Christ in his death and resurrection. United with him in his death, the death of the believer is transformed. This profound truth is central to the science of salvation. Think about that teaching: the Christian is *united* with Christ in his very death. We *join with* Christ in his death. Created, body and soul, in the image and likeness of God, and united with the Lord in Baptism, the Christian's body is marked as a temple of the Holy Spirit. This is why we regard the body, the earthly remains of the deceased, with reverence and honor. The body is sprinkled with holy water to recall Baptism, and it is reverenced with incense, for it has been sealed with the sign of the cross. Because of the transformation in Christ experienced in and through the sacraments, the body of the deceased points to and awaits the resurrection of the dead.

When I reached out and touched the hand of my friend's father, I touched *more* than his hand. I had reached beyond, in some way, *into* the mystery of Christ. That is why it has taken so long for me to begin to understand it. When we view the mortal remains of the deceased Christian, we stand in the presence of an extraordinary mystery. By dying, Christ has united himself with the death of every person. And so, as painful as it is, when we stand and confront the remains of the deceased believer, we are doing much more than saying "goodbye." We are in the presence of a sign that points directly to the death of the Lord. At their deepest level the rituals associated with grief and mourning contain a far-deeper significance: Christian death is a participation in the death of the Lord. Amid the deep sorrow we feel when we lose someone we love, a light shines through. Faith leads us to detect the fundamental importance of this light. Though seen through eyes filled with tears, its brightness transforms the painful customs associated with burial into openings that remind us of the mystery of Christ's own saving descent among the dead.

CHAPTER TEN

————❧❧❧————

Jesus and the Resurrection:
God's Own Joy

After Jesus' lifeless body had been taken down from the cross, Mary Magdalene, Salome, and Mary, the mother of James, did not have time to anoint it for burial (see Mk 16:1). *The final cruelty*: they were denied even the customary farewell and the preparation of the body for the tomb. So they planned to return after the Sabbath to anoint Jesus' body. Everything was rushed. On Good Friday, time itself had run away from the Lord and those he loved.

On the other hand, like everything else in these last few hours, time seems to be on the side of the chief priest and Pharisees. In fact, they *take their time*. But on the Sabbath, the chief priest and Pharisees go to Pilate to ask that the tomb be guarded (see Mt 27:62–64). Saint Thomas notes that Pilate, by his thorough review, unwittingly assures testimony to the saving truth; he diligently offers final certification of the Lord's death on the cross.[1] No one

---

1. See *STh* IIIa, q 51 a 1.

can later claim that the Lord had not died on the cross. Pilate allows the tomb to be guarded (see Mt 27:66) and he tells them to go and *secure* (*asphalizō*) it. Curiously, at the same time, he tells them to *see* (*eidō*), *watch* or *observe* the tomb. Irony abounds. Pilate is an unknowing evangelist. He testifies to the death of the Lord and now he tells the world to watch the tomb.

After the Sabbath, the Lord's friends went, to carry out the human custom of preparing Jesus' body for burial—or so they thought. They set off in the darkness of the early morning of the third day (see Jn 20:1). It is as if every person who has ever been baffled by death shuffled forward in bewilderment and pain with the women on this narrow, dark road. When they reached the tomb they found a very large boulder blocking their path (see Mt 27:60; Mk 15:46; Jn 20:1). The narrow maze of life and death appears closed in on itself. The thread we have been following disappears beneath the terrible boulder. All we can do now is weep (see Jn 20:11). The path is finished. It is easy for us to feel this way when we lose those we love. I have felt this way as I have tried over the years to think about the mystery of death. Death seems impossible to understand, like a large, immovable boulder.

But God interrupts, which is to say he erupts. As the women were on their way to the tomb, an earthquake occurred (see Mt 28:2). This aftershock of Calvary was a harbinger of the magnitude of heaven's gifts. An angel of the Lord descended. It was as if the angel, stilled on Holy Thursday evening in Gethsemane, was finally permitted to release his fury, but on the tomb instead of the mob in the garden. The angel rolled back the stone and then, in full victory, rested upon it. The stone was the very thing that stood in the way. It was the worrisome, immovable, looming obstacle. But the faithful women did not turn back but kept moving toward the obstacle. They had come to touch the body of the Lord in a moment of final ritual, and their moment of seeming defeat was transformed. They were privileged to witness the appearance of the angel and to observe the empty tomb. In a further reversal, the guards, those *outside* the tomb, fell down like dead men (see Mt 28:4). The thread leads us forward.

The empty tomb

The garden of the resurrection holds precious clues we must closely examine. First, as we have seen, each of the four evangelists testifies that the women find the stone rolled away. Second, the tomb, "the place where he lay" (Mt 28:6), is now empty. His body is not there. The objection is easily raised that the empty tomb and the absence of Jesus' mortal remains can be explained by the theft of the body. However, at least two pieces of evidence ensure that the body was not stolen. First, the tomb was under constant surveillance by the enemies of Jesus. The chief priests and the Pharisees were very concerned that the disciples would steal the body and then claim the Lord had risen (see Mt 27:62–63). After going to the lengths they had to attempt to destroy the Lord, they would never have allowed the tomb to be unguarded even for a moment. Guards secured and watched it constantly (see Mt 27:65). Second, those with even a scant motive to steal the body, the disciples of the Lord, were cowering with fear. They had run from Gethsemane in terror for their lives (see Mt 26:56; Mk 14:50–52). They had denied knowing the Lord (see Mt 26:69–75; Mk 14:66–72; Lk 22:54–62; Jn 18:15–18; 25–27). If they had been so quickly terrified when the Lord was alive, then surely after he had died their fear would have increased. They would never have approached a tomb, much less a guarded tomb. They must have felt lost in a maze that was revolving and turning upside down. They were so devastated and confused that they locked themselves away for another week—even after the Risen Lord had appeared to them (see Jn 20:26). It is simply impossible that these men, overcome with such paralyzing fear, could have stolen the body. While the empty tomb is not direct proof of the resurrection, it is, in the context of the events that surround it, a sign of Jesus' complete victory over sin and death.

The appearances of the risen Lord

We find a third precious clue in the report of the angelic messenger that Jesus has been raised from the dead (see Mt 28:5–6; Mk 16:4–6; Lk 24:2–7; Jn 20:1–18). The angel announces, "Do not be afraid; I know that you are looking for Jesus who was crucified. He is not here; for he has been raised, as he said. Come, see the place where he lay" (Mt 28:5–6). Christ is alive. Those who were sent to guard the tomb appear to be dead (see Mt 28:4). The tomb is empty—and humanity begins to search again for God. Before sin and the Fall, when Adam and Eve searched for God they always *found* him. The searching *was* the finding and the finding *was* the searching. In sin, the search and finding is disrupted and delayed. When God searched for Adam and Eve after they sinned, they hid from God. Even their attempt to hide is a type of inverse search for God. And so, God assisted them and called out, "Where are you?" (Gn 3:9). It is easy to imagine God saying to us, "Where are you?" in a corrective tone as if to point out that we have done something wrong. But perhaps we should imagine God saying these words in a tragically heartbroken searching for us. The search God began in the Garden of Eden deepened in the Garden of Gethsemane. As Jesus addresses the mob that had come with torches and clubs, he calls out again to man, "Whom are you looking for?" (Jn 18:4). And now, that search culminates in the garden of the resurrection. Saint Thomas emphasizes that the Lord's burial in a garden shows that humanity is delivered from the sin which was committed in the garden of paradise.[2] In a sense, the three gardens—Eden, Gethsemane, and that of the resurrection—are the same garden: the one in which we search for God and God searches for us. The Lord always longs to be found.

Early on Easter morning, Saint Mary Magdalene searches for the Lord in this garden. The maze of death was already contorted and confusing for her, but now, as she encounters the Lord's tomb, it seems to narrow more and more, closing in on her and collapsing. Weeping, she peers into the opening of the tomb (see Jn 20:11). Our age-old search for God now sounds with profound and untold depths. From inside the tomb the angels ask her why she weeps. She responds, "They have taken away my Lord and I do not know where they have laid him" (Jn 20:13). In her search for the Lord, the tears that fall from her eyes come from her heart.

The tears we shed for a loved one's passing are windows that permit us a fleeting glimpse of the contours of eternity. The Son's cry from the cross, "My God, my God, why have you forsaken me?" (Mt 27:46), echoes throughout all time, and Mary's tears are the silent answer. The angels become hushed spectators of the drama before them. The Lord's cry has cracked the imposing walls of the maze of death. Mary turns and sees Jesus. In this passage Mary's repeated "turning" is a type of prayer. She is searching for Jesus.[3] She does not yet recognize him. She supposes the man she encounters to be the gardener. She is inching closer. God was Eden's gardener: "the Lord God planted a garden in Eden, in the east" (Gn 2:8). With one question: "Whom are you looking for?" (Jn 20:15), the dreadful walls of the maze now totter. Mary's search is insistent: "Sir, if you have carried him away, tell me where you have laid him, and I will

---

2. See *STh* IIIa, q 51, a 2.

3. See Henri De Lubac, *A Brief Catechesis on Nature and Grace*, 121, n. 5.

take him away" (Jn 20:15). The walls of the maze of death collapse, give way, fall back, and disappear: "Jesus said to her, 'Mary!' She turned and said to him in Hebrew, 'Rabbouni!' (which means Teacher).... Mary Magdalene went and announced to the disciples, 'I have seen the Lord'; and she told them that he had said these things to" (Jn 20:16, 18). The maze is transformed forever into the building blocks of the new and eternal Jerusalem. The Lord is risen!

The Gospels do not tell us of any eyewitnesses to the actual event of the resurrection of Jesus, nor do they describe how the resurrection took place. But they do tell us about several incidents in which many witnesses testify to a real encounter with the risen Jesus. They report that the risen Jesus appeared first to Saint Mary Magdalene (see Jn 20:15; Mk 16:9). Then he appeared to the eleven apostles while they were at table (see Mk 16:14), and again when they were on the Mount of the Ascension (see Mt 28:16–20; Mk 16:19–20; Lk 24:50–53). Later the risen Jesus also appeared to two of the disciples (see Mk 16:12–13).

The historical record testifies to the truth about the appearances of the risen Lord. So too does the effect of his appearances. The apostles were utterly distraught at his death. Their lives had fallen apart. They were marked men, cowering behind locked doors, afraid to show themselves in public for fear of being arrested and charged. The One in whom they trusted, the One on whom they had staked everything, had died a shameful death at the hands of the religious and civil authorities. And, since they were known to be his followers, they would be next. If they had run away and hid at the prospect of his death, the prospect of their own death would have sent them deeper into hiding.

Yet, we have many records testifying to the fact that only a few days after Jesus' death, these same men were now boldly proclaiming the risen Lord. During Saint Peter's speech on Pentecost, he says, "This Jesus God raised up, and of that all of us are witnesses" (Acts

2:32). What changed the apostles from scared deniers to fearless witnesses? It was their real encounter with the risen Lord. The early Christian community solidly attests to the reality of the appearances of the risen Jesus: "After his suffering he presented himself alive to them by many convincing proofs, appearing to them during forty days and speaking about the kingdom of God" (Acts 1:3, see 1:22). The witness continues: "But God raised him on the third day and allowed him to appear, not to all the people but to us who were chosen by God as witnesses, and who ate and drank with him after he rose from the dead. He commanded us to preach to the people and to testify that he is the one ordained by God as judge of the living and the dead" (Acts 10:40–42). Saint Paul likewise underwent a profound transformation from a persecutor of the Church to its courageous missionary:

> For I handed on to you as of first importance what I in turn had received: that Christ died for our sins in accordance with the scriptures, and that he was buried, and that he was raised on the third day in accordance with the scriptures, and that he appeared to Cephas, then to the twelve. Then he appeared to more than five hundred brothers and sisters[a] at one time, most of whom are still alive, though some have died. Then he appeared to James, then to all the apostles. Last of all, as to one untimely born, he appeared also to me. (1 Cor 15:3–8; see Acts 9:1–19; 5–16; 26:10–18)

With their own eyes they saw him alive whom they had known to be dead. And this transforms the apostles and the disciples into people of daring faith. Yet the appearances also convey to us important facts about the nature of the resurrection.

The Road to Emmaus

The appearances of the risen Lord also reveal further clues about the resurrection. Saint Luke relates the appearance on the road to

Emmaus, which takes place on Easter Sunday itself (see Lk 24:13–35). Two of the Lord's disciples are leaving Jerusalem, going to the village of Emmaus. They were not present at the empty tomb. They have yet to hear any word of the appearance of the risen Lord to Saint Mary Magdalene. The Gospel does not tell us the reason for their journey, but it does give us a clue in relating one seemingly incidental fact. The village of Emmaus was seven miles from Jerusalem. Like the other disciples of Jesus, over the last forty-eight hours these two disciples had experienced the traumatic collapse of everything dear to them. The pain was too much, so they were running away—seven miles away. Seven, the number of completion or perfection, indicates that they wanted to completely distance themselves from all that had happened. They were running away from the confounding maze of death. And, as they ran, ". . . they were talking and discussing, Jesus himself came near and went with them, but their eyes were kept from recognizing him" (Lk 24:15–16).

The two disciples have the same experience as Saint Mary Magdalene. As with Mary, the Lord is visible to the human eye, but the two disciples, who would have been very familiar with the Lord, fail to recognize him. While Saint Mary Magdalene thought he was the gardener, the two disciples on the road think he is a stranger, the "only one" who does not know what has taken place in Jerusalem the past few days. Ironically, Jesus is the only one who really knows the full extent of these events. As he did with Mary that very morning, the Lord speaks to the two disciples. They finally recognize him in the breaking of the bread, but the incomprehensibility returns as he vanishes from their sight. Even so, they truly recognize him all the more: "Were not our hearts burning within us while he was talking to us on the road" (Lk 24:32).

The appearances are consistent; the body of the risen Lord is somehow different. It is clear that Jesus did not return to a passible earthly life as did Jairus' daughter, the son of the widow of Nain, and

Lazarus. Some of those who were very familiar with Jesus fail to recognize him at first. At the same time, something about his body appears *very much the same*. Finally they *do* recognize him and rejoice. The risen Jesus' appearances to the disciples are not simply meditative events or times of mystical prayer. In their external experience, the disciples truly encounter the physical reality of the risen Lord. His body is tangible, able at times to be recognized by the human senses. Yet something about his glorified existence eludes human perception. His risen body manifests additional new properties. He can pass through locked doors (see Jn 20:19), yet he can be touched (see Jn 20:17; Lk 24:39). He can speak, be heard, suddenly appear, and then vanish just as suddenly. He can work miracles and he can eat (see Lk 24:30, 41–43; Jn 21:5, 12–13). Von Balthasar tells us that the appearances of the risen Lord are moments in which eternity is passing through time. Time and eternity are somehow contemporaneous in these moments; there is the objective perception of Jesus' visible presence by those who see him, and yet some elements of eternity are blocked or not fully visible to the eyes of those in time.[4]

The risen Lord appears to the disciples within space and time, yet the characteristics of his glorified body prove that space and time cannot confine him for he has passed beyond them. His body is his real body with new properties. Even though he has passed beyond time and space in his resurrection, the risen Christ, in his humility, now subjects himself to the limits of history and, even as he does so, he points infinitely beyond that same history.[5] His body is not

---

4. See Hans Urs von Balthasar, *A Theology of History* (San Francisco: Ignatius Press, 1994), 85 and *The Glory of the Lord: A Theological Aesthetics I: Seeing the Form* (San Francisco: Ignatius Press, 1989), 200–201, 503–504, and 672–674.

5. See Gustave Martelet, *The Risen Christ and the Eucharistic World* (New York: The Seabury Press, 1976), 93.

confined to the laws of matter as it had been prior to the resurrection, but is now filled with the supernatural power of the Holy Spirit. Christ's humanity, even his body, is perfectly introduced into the communion of the Trinity (*CCC* 646). Having passed into the fullness of glory, the Lord's risen body shares in the glory of the soul (*CCC* 625). The resurrection of Jesus Christ from the dead is an objective and utterly unique act of God, by which God has forever established the message of his Son.[6] The risen body demonstrates the completeness of the resurrection. Everything that had been lost in death is now wondrously restored.[7] The body of the glorified and risen Lord holds an even more precious clue: the wounds of his crucifixion. The Lord invites the apostles to learn the mystery of his resurrection by examining and touching his wounds.

The wounds

The two disciples at Emmaus, after the risen Lord vanishes from their sight, immediately return to Jerusalem. What they had *run from* in fear, they now *run to* out of love. They burst in upon the apostles in hiding and announce that they have seen the Lord. At that point the risen Jesus appears to the disciples in the upper room in Jerusalem. They are terrified and think that he is a ghost. This reaction confirms the pattern: they notice something similar yet different about the glorified body of the Lord. Jesus stills their alarm. He shows proof of his identity: " 'Look at my hands and my feet; see that it is I myself. Touch me and see; for a ghost does not have flesh and bones as you see that I have.' And when he had said this, he showed them his hands and his feet" (Lk 24:39–40). Jesus *shows* the

---

6. See *The Church's Confession of Faith*, 167.
7. See *STh* IIIa, q 54, a 3.

apostles the same body he had before. He shows them the nail wounds and the signs of his sacred passion. He literally holds out his wounds as the way for them to recognize him. He is the very One with whom they had dwelt prior to his crucifixion.

The scars Jesus bears are not signs of deformity, corruption, or defect, but, rather, a brilliant glory shines forth from his sacred wounds.[8] They are an eternal witness: their presence in his glorified body confirms the testimony about him: "The man who appeared to them was *the same* whom they had known previously from a long association and whom they had seen suffer and die."[9] More so, by inviting them to *touch* his wounds, he testifies that his glorified body has flesh and bones. He is no mere hallucination or phantasm. He and his body are real. Those wounds that once wreaked havoc on the Lord's body, even to his death have been transformed in an incredible way.

The Lord's wounds also have the power to transform our own experience of death. When at my first wake my mother touched the hand of the deceased man, I looked up at her and she nodded that I, too, could reach out and touch his hand. It was certainly not the same as the invitation to touch the glorified body of the Lord, but something was at work there. In one sense, every dead body is a wound. It is a sign of one who has fallen into death. The dead body of the Christian is a unique sign, for it was baptized into the death and resurrection of the Lord. The Christian, having hoped in the resurrection, now awaits the fulfillment of the promise. In touching the man's hand, I was also, in some way, touching the living mystery. Jesus has *undergone* death and, through his resurrection, has changed it into a passage to new life. Death, the relentless "last enemy"

---

8. See *STh* IIIa, q 54, a 4.

9. Hans Urs von Balthasar, *The Glory of the Lord I*, 344.

(1 Cor 15:26; see Rev 20:14) and constant burden, has lost its sting. Death is hollowed out and filled with the capacity to make us aware of God's presence. Therefore, death is destroyed forever (see 1 Cor 15:26, 55), and through the love of God, transformed into a new beginning. The death of the Christian is an encounter with Christ in the mystery of his victorious death and resurrection.[10]

In the Gospel of Saint John, the disciples rejoice when the Lord shows them the wounds in his hands and side (see Jn 20:20). Saint Thomas the Apostle was not present then. When he returned, they told him that they had seen the Lord. Thomas did not believe their report. He was so skeptical that he asserted, "Unless I see the mark of the nails in his hands, and put my finger in the mark of the nails and my hand in his side, I will not believe" (Jn 20:25). A week later, Thomas is present with the other apostles when the risen Lord again appears. The Lord says to him, "Put your finger here and see my hands. Reach out your hand and put it in my side. Do not doubt but believe" (Jn 20:27). Thomas answers, "My Lord and my God" (Jn 20:28). Saint Thomas Aquinas tells us that Saint Thomas the Apostle actually touched the wounds of our Lord not for his own personal faith but for us, on our behalf.[11] Not only did Jesus rise with his wounds, but he also invites us to touch his wounds through faith: "Blessed are those who have not seen and yet have come to believe" (Jn 20:29; see Lk 24:39). Von Balthasar emphasizes that the post-resurrection appearances of the risen Lord provide us with, "Superabundant evidence that stretches the

---

10. See Damien Sicard, "Christian Death" in *The Church at Prayer Volume III: The Sacraments* (Minnesota: The Liturgical Press, 1988), 222.

11. See *STh*, IIIa, q 54, a 4, ad 2.

human faculties to the breaking point."[12] The heart of the mystery is this: we can touch the wounds of the Lord, for they are open eternally.[13] He bestows the Holy Spirit through his wounds.[14] In this present life we touch his wounds through faith. Saint Peter reminds us of the promise of faith: "Although you have not seen him, you love him; and even though you do not see him now, you believe in him and rejoice with an indescribable and glorious joy, for you are receiving the outcome of your faith, the salvation of your souls" (1 Pt 1:8–9).

Some claim that the appearances described by the disciples were only hallucinations. Yet, their experience is not consistent with hallucinations. The apostles did not immediately believe the report of the women (see Mk 16:11, 13–14; Lk 24:11; Jn 20:25). At first they did not believe when the risen Lord appeared to them (see Mt 28:17). At first the disciples were doubtful, and Thomas was highly skeptical. They were not likely candidates to have hallucinations. Further, how could a group of out-of-work, irascible fishermen and a tax collector—who had failed at almost everything they tried—be capable of defrauding the human race for over two millennia with a hoax based on a hallucination? To that point the only thing they had ever succeeded in was outrunning one another in fear when they were most needed. When they stopped running *away* and instead *ran to the tomb*, they ran under a new power. Their encounters with the risen Lord changed them into bold and daring proclaimers of the Gospel and Christ's victory over evil and death.

---

12. Hans Urs von Balthasar, *The Glory of the Lord I*, 202.

13. Hans Urs von Balthasar, *Theodrama IV*, 337.

14. Saint John Paul II, *Dominum et vivificantem*, no. 24.

The resurrection

The resurrection of Jesus Christ from the dead is confirmed by those who had direct contact with the risen Lord, an experience verified by their unanimous eyewitness testimony.[15] The resurrection is a real and objective historical event. While it stands above history, it has truly occurred within history.[16] The resurrection of Jesus from the dead establishes an utterly new dimension of existence that involves the fullness of physical, bodily existence. Just as death fully impacted Jesus' existence, so too does the resurrection. It is not simply restitution for what happened on the cross. The resurrection is the *fruit* of the cross and the wellspring from which the Spirit is lavished, from Jesus, onto the Church.[17] Christ completely overcame death, which is now excluded forever. His risen body is the origin, principle, and source of the transformation of the universe to life without end. Death can no longer prevent all the great promises of life: "We know that Christ, being raised from the dead, will never die again; death no longer has dominion over him. The death he died, he died to sin, once and for all; but the life he lives, he lives to God. So you also must consider yourselves dead to sin and alive to God in Christ Jesus" (Rom 6:9–11).

Our resurrection

The empty tomb and the appearances of the risen Lord are not simply arguments meant to convince the skeptical. They are *gifts of*

---

15. See Saint John Paul II, *Jesus, Son and Savior*, 490–491.

16. See Pope Benedict XVI, *Jesus of Nazareth Part II*, loc 3466 and 3483 of 4202; see also Gustave Martelet, *The Risen Christ and the Eucharistic World*, 90.

17. See Louis Bouyer, *The Spirituality of the New Testament and the Fathers*, 59, 196.

love by which the Lord not only shows us his victory over sin and death, but also promises to *share that same victory with us*. Christ's resurrection is *the source of our own future resurrection*. The Prophet Hosea foretold it long ago: "After two days he will revive us; on the third day he will raise us up" (Hos 6:2). Saint Paul tells us, "But in fact Christ has been raised from the dead, the first fruits of those who have died. For since death came through a human being, the resurrection of the dead has also come through a human being; for as all die in Adam, so all will be made alive in Christ" (1 Cor 15:20–22). Paul repeats: Christ is "the firstborn from the dead" (Col 1:18), "the firstborn among many brothers" (Rom 8:29 NABRE). The Apostle to the Gentiles further testifies: "For if we have been united with him in a death like his, we will certainly be united with him in a resurrection like his" (Rom 6:5). We have come upon the great and central truth of Christianity: Jesus has passed from death to eternal life. The first of those raised from the dead, Jesus extends to us a share in his resurrection. Saint John tells us that those who rise with Christ "will be like him" (1 Jn 3:2). Saint Paul further explains that this sharing comes through the Spirit of Christ dwelling within us: "If the Spirit of him who raised Jesus from the dead dwells in you, he who raised Christ from the dead will give life to your mortal bodies also through his Spirit that dwells in you" (Rom 8:11).

We begin to share in the resurrection of Christ through the sacraments. Baptism begins our initiation into the cross of Jesus. As the Baptismal ceremony opens, the one to be baptized is signed with the cross on his or her forehead. During the Baptism itself, they are either plunged beneath the water or the water is poured over them three times. The threefold pouring or immersion represents the three days that Jesus was in the tomb. This is the great and primary effect of Baptism: it joins us permanently to Jesus Christ in his saving death and glorious resurrection. Saint Paul emphasizes this: "Do you not know that all of us who have been baptized into Christ

Jesus were baptized into his death? Therefore we have been buried with him by baptism into death, so that, just as Christ was raised from the dead by the glory of the Father, so we too might walk in newness of life" (Rom 6:3–4). Saint Paul wishes to know "nothing except Jesus Christ, and him crucified" (1 Cor 2:2). The other effects of Baptism flow from this primary effect: original sin is forgiven because the presence of Christ banishes sin, and we are made members of his body the Church, since where Christ is, so is his Church. We now share in the life and gifts of the Holy Spirit.

The Holy Eucharist is the culmination and great foretaste of our sharing in the resurrection of Christ: "Those who eat my flesh and drink my blood have eternal life, and I will raise them up on the last day" (Jn 6:54). Saint Ignatius of Antioch refers to the Eucharist as the "medicine of immortality and the antidote that we should not die but live forever in Jesus Christ."[18] As we live the life of faith, we await the fulfillment of Christ's promise. No aspect of the Christian life is arbitrary. The sacraments, the life of grace and virtue, vocation, prayer, and the practice of the works of mercy are all essential. Yet these are each grounded in the essential fact of the resurrection of Jesus from the dead: "if Christ has not been raised, then our proclamation has been in vain and your faith has been in vain" (1 Cor 15:14).

The victory of Jesus Christ culminates in Easter, but it does not end there. During the forty days after Easter, the risen Lord prepares the apostles for the mission he entrusts to his Church. The Lord's victorious death is now to be proclaimed until the end of the world (see 1 Cor 11:26).

---

18. Saint Ignatius of Antioch, *Letter to the Ephesians*, *The Apostolic Fathers*, trans. J. B. Lightfoot (New York: Macmillan, 1891), 142.

The ascension

The appearances of the risen Lord form the apostles for the mission he entrusts to them. Forty days after Easter the Lord leads his apostles to the scene of his final appearance. "Then he led them out as far as Bethany, and, lifting up his hands, he blessed them. While he was blessing them, he withdrew from them and was carried up into heaven" (Lk 24:50–51; see Acts 1:3; 6–12).

We can easily slip into thinking that the ascension is a kind of "final act" or finale. But the ascension is not a termination. It is quite the opposite. As Jesus "goes away" from us into heaven, he actually becomes *closer* and *more accessible* to us in every time and place through his Church. The ascension is the sign that the Lord's presence is now invisible and beyond time. Von Balthasar explains that with the ascension the Lord shows his disciples, in a direct and concrete way, the reality in which he will remain with them to the end of the world (see Mt 28:20).[19] Saint Thomas Aquinas emphasizes that the Lord ascends so as to increase our faith in things unseen, to strengthen our hope for heaven, and to guide our charity toward the things of heaven.[20] Already during his public ministry the Lord had promised: "And I, when I am lifted up from the earth, will draw all people to myself" (Jn 12:32). The definitive "lifting up" that took place on the cross is now fulfilled in the ascension of the Lord. The Lord is "taken up into heaven" (Mk 16:19); he passes into heavenly glory with his promise to return (see Acts 1:11).

---

19. See Hans Urs von Balthasar, *A Theology of History*, 87.
20. See *Summa Theologiae* IIIa, q 57, a 1, ad 3.

Seen in this light, the ascension is also *an event of our salvation.* It is an action of the priesthood of Christ. As he ascends, Jesus does so in his glorified humanity. The humanity of Jesus does not evaporate or dissolve, nor is it absorbed into his divinity. Jesus retains his humanity, the true flesh he assumed in the womb of our Lady. "In his resurrection he resumed unto an everlasting life, the body which in his conception he had assumed to a mortal life."[21] The ascension is the crowning of the entire work of redemption and it is a sign of the destiny of all those united to Christ.[22] The humanity of Christ, crucified and risen, now enters into the divine glory of heaven so that he may intercede for us at the right hand of the Father (see Rom 8:34; Col 3:1; Eph 1:20; Ps 110:1). The ascension is the decisive moment in which the Lord has eternally opened up a space in God for humanity.[23]

Long ago the psalmist hinted at the deep mystery within the ascension: "Lift up your heads, O gates! and be lifted up, O ancient doors! that the King of glory may come in. Who is the King of glory? The LORD, strong and mighty, the LORD, mighty in war" (Ps 24:7–8). This verse is attributed to the angelic hosts. At the ascension, the angels in heaven see the Victor approaching the heavenly gates. At first *they almost fail to recognize him.* How can the myriad of angels not recognize the eternal Son? Because in his saving mission he has joined human nature to himself in the Incarnation, and now he approaches in his risen, glorified body. He bears the glorious wounds. The indescribable splendor of Christ, crucified and risen,

---

21. *Summa Theologiae* IIIa, q 54, a 3.

22. See Louis Bouyer, *The Meaning of the Monastic Life*, 24–27, 33 and 42.

23. See Pope Benedict XVI, *Jesus of Nazareth Part II Holy Week: From the Entrance into Jerusalem to the Resurrection*, loc 3624 of 4202.

ascending in triumph to the Father, fills the angels with untold wonder. At first they can only marvel at his magnificent brilliance. When they do recognize him they acclaim, "Let him enter, the king of glory!" The Lord enters heaven and opens the house of the Father. Where he has gone, we hope to follow.

The ascension has not only a heavenly meaning, but also a meaning quite down to earth. The power of the ascension propels the Church outward in evangelization and mission. Just prior to his ascension Jesus says to his followers:

> "All authority in heaven and on earth has been given to me. Go therefore and make disciples of all nations, baptizing them in the name of the Father and of the Son and of the Holy Spirit, and teaching them to obey everything that I have commanded you. And remember, I am with you always, to the end of the age." (Mt 28:18–20)

As Jesus ascends into heaven, he sends the Church forth on earth. The ascension sparks something new: as Jesus ascends in exaltation to the right hand of the Father, together they send the Holy Spirit upon the apostles. The Lord had told the apostles, "if I do not go away, the Advocate will not come to you; but if I go, I will send him to you" (Jn 16:7). Jesus himself founded the Church and conferred its leadership on Saint Peter (see Mt 16: 18–19; Jn 21:15–19), the first pope. The sacred passion of the Lord, his saving death, glorious resurrection, ascension into heaven, and conferral of the Holy Spirit at Pentecost are all part of the same continuous mystery.

It is important to point out that the ascension of our Lord differs from the teaching on the assumption of our Lady into heaven. The assumption refers to the passing of the Blessed Virgin Mary, body and soul, into heaven at the end of her earthly life. Her body does not experience the decay of death. The archangel Gabriel described her as full of grace (see Lk 1:28). Each generation proclaims her blessedness (see Lk 1:48). She is the sinless Mother of God's only-begotten Son. As such, it is fitting that she share, body and soul, in her Son's heavenly glory. The Queen of Heaven always points to our final goal. Her bodily glorification is a sign and anticipation of all who will share the glory of heaven.[24]

---

24. See Sacred Congregation for the Doctrine of the Faith, *Letter on Certain Questions Concerning Eschatology* May 17, 1979: *AAS* 71 (1979), 941.

CHAPTER ELEVEN

The Last Things

History intrigues us. Academic study, popular books, and documentaries explore history's epochal moments. We never seem to tire of thinking about our past. Ultimately, history and science team up, attempting to reach back so as to scratch the surface of human origins. Yet, sadly, people today dedicate less and less time to considering our ultimate future, where we are going. While we can learn from the past, we cannot change it. Yet, we can influence and affect our future. Attentive in some measure to our past, and often vague about our future destiny, the present moment is the decisive time that consolidates the past and forges its many lessons into wisdom so as to transform the future. In the present moment we hold fast to the sturdy thread of faith.

Now, we turn another corner and face the future. We turn to places where none of us on earth have been: the particular judgment, hell, purgatory, heaven, and the general judgment. These have traditionally been called the last things. As we step forward in humility and awe, we hold fast to and renew our fidelity to Christ and the authentic teaching of his Church, for "Good and upright is the LORD; therefore he instructs sinners in the way. He leads the humble in what is right, and teaches the humble his way. . . . He will teach them the way that they should choose" (Ps 25:8–9, 12).

The particular judgment

All the questions asked in this book have flowed from the question I had at age ten. My ultimate question then is humanity's ultimate question: What *happens* to us when we die? Death is the separation of soul and body. We know what happens to the body at death. The Church teaches that "a spiritual element survives and subsists after death, an element endowed with consciousness and will, so that the 'human self' subsists" though it lacks the completion of its body.[1] What happens to the soul at the moment of death? Where does it go?

We make choices every day, ultimate choices between good and evil, sin and grace. The Church guides us to discern and follow the will of God in all things, to choose the path of virtue and goodness. Through his Church, God offers us countless opportunities every hour to turn to faith, hope, and love; to a life of prudence, justice, fortitude, and temperance. In his grace God offers us the opportunity, even up to the moment of death, to turn from evil ways. In this present life God always invites us to respond through grace to his free offer of redemption and salvation. Therefore, we cannot be judged until after we die. At death the choices for good or evil we have made during our life become fixed.[2]

---

1. Sacred Congregation for the Doctrine of the Faith, *Letter on Certain Questions Concerning Eschatology* May 17, 1979: *AAS* 71 (1979), 941. See also *DS* 4653.

2. See Pope Benedict XVI, *Spe Salvi*, no. 45. See also Saint Catherine of Genoa, *Purgation and Purgatory* as in *Catherine of Genoa, Purgation and Purgatory, The Spiritual Dialogue* The Classics of Western Spirituality (New Jersey: Paulist Press, 1979), 74.

The Church teaches that God judges the human person immediately at the moment of death. In the twenty-first century, particularly in the West, we are not used to hearing the word "judgment" in a positive light. We are more familiar with compromise, with making deals, or with bargaining. But love is never a bargain or a deal. Love does not compromise things away. Judgment is a confirmation, a follow-through, the perfection of the intellect. The Letter to the Hebrews tells us, "It is appointed for mortals to die once, and after that the judgment" (Heb 9:27). Saint Paul likewise says, "For we will all stand before the judgment seat of God" (Rom 14:10). The judgment that takes place at the moment of death is called the particular judgment. It is called "particular" because at that moment each individual person stands before God and is judged in accordance with his or her deeds and faith (*CCC* 1021). We do not just review our "record" of "do's and don'ts."

The human being is created in the image and likeness of God and redeemed by the blood of Jesus. Therefore, this judgment is based ultimately on Jesus Christ: "He is the one ordained by God as judge of the living and the dead" (Acts 10:42). Saint Peter teaches, "But they will have to give an accounting to him who stands ready to judge the living and the dead" (1 Pt 4:5). And Saint Paul reminds us, "For all of us must appear before the judgment seat of Christ, so that each may receive recompense for what has been done in the body, whether good or evil" (2 Cor 5:10; see Rom 14:10). Something wondrous happens at the particular judgment: all speculation vanishes and we finally see our entire life *in light of the truth of Jesus Christ*. He is our Advocate who pleads our cause. But love always abides in freedom. Love does not reverse or turn back the free and deliberate choices we have made as regards Christ and his offer of grace. At the particular judgment each person, in his or her immortal soul, receives immediately his or her eternal reward or punishment. The just enter heaven; those who need purification enter purgatory to be purified of the obstacles to their receiving their eternal reward in heaven; the damned enter hell.

The particular judgment is the moment for which we spend our entire lives preparing. The foremost preparation takes place in the sacraments. Baptism, Confirmation, and the Holy Eucharist infallibly *introduce us to Christ*. These sacraments of initiation begin and nourish the life of grace within us. Indelibly joined to Christ, we still experience temptation and the onslaught of evil (see 2 Thes 2:7; 1 Cor 7:26; Eph 5:16; 1 Pet 4:17). Our freedom remains and includes the possibility that we, though joined to our Lord through his grace, may make the tragic choice to freely do evil. Every evil choice is painful to the human soul. The definitive and most dreadful form of evil is mortal sin. This sin is the free and deliberate choice to oppose God in a serious matter with full consent of the will and sufficient reflection. Mortal sin kills the life of sanctifying grace in the soul. Even in this most heartrending of sins, the Lord continues to summon us to repentance so that we may again share deeply in his life. He never ceases to invite us to follow the call to holiness and live a life of virtue. The sacrament of Penance is the only ordinary means by which the Lord forgives mortal sin. Therefore, it is crucial that a person in the state of mortal sin confess those sins in the sacrament of Penance at the first opportunity.

Venial sins are offenses in lesser matters, or in serious matters in which we act without full consent of the will or sufficient reflection (*CCC* 1855, 1862). These sins wound and weaken, but do not completely destroy the life of sanctifying grace in the soul. Venial sins remain a great concern, however, because, if deliberate and unrepented, they can lead us to mortal sin (*CCC* 1863). The regular confession of venial sins in the sacrament of Penance strengthens the consciences and fortifies the life of charity in the soul.

Regular reception of the sacraments of Penance and the Eucharist bring us ever more deeply into the life of grace. The sacraments conform us to Christ so that we may live a holy life in this world and be prepared to meet God directly at the moment of death. Sadly, it may happen that a person does not approach the sacrament of Penance and remains in mortal sin. By the person's own choice, he or she remains cut off from God. Receiving the sacraments in preparation for death is of singular and utmost importance for all, but especially anyone in mortal sin.

For everyone, three sacraments are of central importance in one's last moments on earth. The first is the final absolution received in the sacrament of Penance. Every Catholic should regularly receive this sacrament, but the opportunity to confess one's sins to a priest as death approaches is a moment of unparalleled grace. It is not always possible for the dying person to make auricular Confession, that is, to confess verbally his or her sins to the priest. The person may be physically prevented from speaking or may be in a public context such as an emergency room. In such circumstances, and to ensure that the opportunity for receiving the sacrament is not lost, the priest-confessor may use a general formula to help the person indicate sorrow for sin. In fact, in an emergency, it is sufficient that the dying person simply indicate in the affirmative that they are sorry for all the sins of their past life in order to receive final absolution.

The second sacrament one ought to receive in preparation for death is the Anointing of the Sick. This sacrament is meant also for those who are ill or of advanced age, to strengthen them, heal them, and to consecrate their sufferings as a reminder of the sufferings of Christ. The Church also celebrates this sacrament for those who are close to death for these same reasons: for their spiritual healing, the configuration of their sufferings to those of the Lord, and the forgiveness of sins.

The third sacrament that one receives in preparation for death is the Holy Eucharist received as *viaticum*. The Council of Nicea (325) emphasized the importance of the Eucharist and its connection to our journey to heaven.[3] The Eucharist, the real presence of Christ, is the sacred and heavenly food that strengthens the believer for the final journey into eternal life. These three sacraments are the ordinary manner in which the believer, at the last hour, unites his or her own death to the death of the Lord. These three sacraments prepare the Catholic to meet Christ in the particular judgment.

The holy rosary has a special relationship to Christian death. Those who gather to comfort the dying pray the rosary so as to entrust them to the protection of the Mother of God. Just as she was present at the death of her Son, the Mother of the Lord is present at the death of each believer. She comforts us and guides us to her Son, whose numberless mercies she seeks to lovingly administer in our final moments.[4]

The expression "Last Rites," while not as commonly used today, expresses the urgency associated with our final preparation to meet God. But we need not focus exclusively on the word "Last," which could generate panic and alarm. The celebration of the sacraments when death nears is an enduring beacon of hope and light, not a gloomy harbinger of doom. But because it was sometimes seen in that negative way, the tendency developed to defer calling the priest as a person neared death. As death approaches, profound emotions and strong feelings easily arise. Yet the sacraments are the action of God by which he casts the light of his grace deep into our hearts, so that Jesus may accompany us even in the most difficult moments. Preparing for a good death is part of living a good life.

---

3. See *DS* 129.
4. See Hans Urs von Balthasar, *Theodrama V: The Last Act*, 345.

Hell

God created us so that we could share God's very life of love. In original sin, we turned away from God's gift of love. God the Father reached out from the depths of Triune love and sent his Son as our Redeemer and bestowed the Holy Spirit to be our special Advocate. Still, we are free. We can decide to deliberately and permanently turn away from the embrace of God's perfect love. Unrepentant mortal sin at the moment of death has an eternal effect on the soul. Hell is the final and definitive consequence of unrepentant mortal sin. The Church teaches that human beings who, of their own free will, permanently reject the endless mercy of God and die in final impenitence, outside of the grace of God, in the state of mortal sin go immediately to hell after death (see Lk 16:22–23; *CCC* 1033). The Book of Genesis, when it describes creation, does not describe hell. This is because hell was "prepared for the devil and his angels" (Mt 25:41). Human beings who die in final and definitive rejection of God's offer of redemption enter this state of eternal separation from God (see Mk 9:42–48).

Several times throughout his public ministry Jesus refers to the pain of eternal separation from God. He speaks more than once of "unquenchable fire" (Mt 3:12; see Mt 25:41; Mk 9:48) and of fiery Gehenna (see Mt 5:22; 23:15, 33). Gehenna was located in the valley of Hinnom to the southwest of Jerusalem, which was used to burn rubbish. Father John Saward points out that in Old Testament times, it was a place where the Canaanites offered the absolute depravity of child sacrifice to Moloch and his idols (see Jer 7:31; 2 Kgs 16:3).[5] The Lord again refers to hell in describing the last day:

---

5. See John Saward, *Sweet and Blessed Country: The Christian Hope for Heaven* (New York: Oxford University Press, 2005), 97.

"Then he will say to those at his left hand, 'You that are accursed, depart from me into the eternal fire prepared for the devil and his angels'" (Mt 25:41). Gehenna, or hell, is, therefore, the place of eternal damnation for those who, of their own free will, have deliberately rejected Christ and died in the state of obstinate and unrepentant mortal sin. The Book of Revelation also speaks of unquenchable burning (see Rev 14:10; 19:20; 20:10; 21:8). Saint Pope John Paul II explained that the image of fire signifies "the complete frustration and emptiness of life without God."[6]

Jesus uses other images to describe eternal separation from God. He warns his disciples of the "outer darkness, where there will be weeping and gnashing of teeth" (Mt 8:12; see 13:50). He also cautions, "Do not fear those who kill the body but cannot kill the soul; rather fear him who can destroy both soul and body in hell" (Mt 10:28). Saint Paul speaks of the punishment to be inflicted on "those who do not know God and on those who do not obey the gospel of our Lord Jesus." The Apostle to the Gentiles is clear that the unrepentant "will suffer the punishment of eternal destruction, separated from the presence of the Lord and from the glory of his might" (2 Thes 1:8–9; 2:10, and 2 Cor 2:15; 4:3). Saint Paul further names certain grave sins that merit eternal separation from God (see 1 Cor 6:9–10; Gal 5:20–21; Eph 5:5) and emphasizes that for all who "live as enemies of the cross of Christ. . . . Their end is destruction" (Phil 3:18–19; see 1 Cor 1:18). Popular images of hell describe it as a place of fire underneath the earth. Saint John Paul II noted, "Rather than a place, hell indicates the state of those who freely and definitively separate themselves from God, the source of all life and joy."[7]

---

6. Saint John Paul II, *The Trinity's Embrace*, 232.
7. Ibid.

Prudent fear of eternal separation from God is very important to the life of the soul. Many people today seem to take little account of the life of the soul. The illusions of temptation easily capture our attention and we may devote more and more of our energies to the things of the world. Even as we carefully provide for family, help our neighbors, and honor our commitments, we all too easily make compromises with sin. So often the modern conscience is not only numb, but also seems to have been working in reverse for the past several generations. People seem to accept that sin is somehow okay or even mainstream. Actions that previous generations considered to be vices and weaknesses are now actively pursued. Greed seems accepted as a natural part of business, along with lying, cheating, and self-centered ambition. Lust has become part of entertainment and recreation. Gossip and trashing someone else's reputation is part of everyday conversation. Revenge and anger become ordinary, and envy is the guide to getting ahead. Pride fits naturally with survival of the fittest. Marriage and family are now disposable. It used to be that the home was the center of people's lives. They went to work in order to provide for a place for their family. Now the home is often merely a terminal, a hotel that people pass through on their way to something more important as they clutch some fast food and rush past those they love. Most horrifyingly, people show less and less regard for the inviolable dignity of human life. Abortion, euthanasia, and physician-assisted suicide are viewed as lifestyle choices rather than murder. Child abuse and neglect are likewise terrible sins that cry to heaven. The daily prejudice of racial injustice destroys the life of charity in the soul. Lack of respect for the Lord's Day and the Holy Name seem commonplace.

Even though it may seem that people sin with little or no regret, each such choice does grave injury to the life of one's soul. Such serious sins imperil a person's eternal salvation. As noted, the only ordinary means for the forgiveness of mortal sin is in the sacrament of Penance. Yet, many people often forget this sacrament of mercy and disregard the injunction of the Lord himself to his Church: "If you forgive the sins of any, they are forgiven them; if you retain the sins of any, they are retained" (Jn 20:23). All the while, we know not the day nor the hour (see Mt 24:36; 25:13, Mk 13:32) when we will be called in a fleeting moment to face God.

Of course, God is infinitely good and all merciful. He does not want anyone to suffer eternal damnation. Those who freely reject God's grace in this present life judge and condemn themselves for all eternity to be deprived of the vision of God (*CCC* 679). The definitive rejection of God becomes irrevocable after the moment of death.[8] The Lord warns his disciples, "For the gate is wide and the road is easy that leads to destruction, and there are many who take it" (Mt 7:13–14). God does not impose hell on anyone, but a person chooses it by the decisions he or she makes during life. God's love only heightens the tragedy that a person may ultimately choose to freely, deliberately, and definitively reject God's offer of salvation. God is love (see 1 Jn 4:8), and, as such, he does not override human freedom or forcibly dispel the choices a person makes: "Eternal damnation remains a real possibility, but we are not granted, without special divine revelation, the knowledge of whether or which human beings are effectively involved in it."[9] The awareness of the existence of hell should turn the mind of believers not to despair, but to seek

---

8. See Pope Benedict XVI, *Spe Salvi*, 45.

9. Saint John Paul II, *The Trinity's Embrace*, 233; see also Germain Grisez and Peter F. Ryan, S.J., "Hell and Hope for Salvation," *New Blackfriars,* vol. 95, issue 1059 (Sept. 2014): 606–15; and Hans Urs von Balthasar, *Dare We Hope "That All Men Be Saved"?* (San Francisco: Ignatius Press, 1988), 166 and 237; and his *Explorations in Theology V: Man is Created*, 344 and 391. Finally, see Cardinal Avery Dulles, "The Population of Hell" *First Things* May 2003.

deeper refuge in Christ: "For the saints, 'hell' is not so much a threat to be hurled at other people but a challenge to oneself."[10]

Purgatory

Human frailty is not a fantasy. It is a daily and often hourly reality. Human beings are weak, and even the best of intentions come under attack from the world. Our spiritual strength can easily fade. We only need examine our own conscience to see that you and I have the tendency to commit daily sins against charity, which are often painful, reactive choices we make without sufficient reflection or full consent of the will. These are the chronic, ingrained, and all-but-intangible self-centered ways that we have tried thousands of times to change on our own. Dozens of times a day we react hurriedly with impatience, self-centeredness, and a quick temper. If we retain these imperfections at the moment of death, we do not merit the penalty of eternal separation from God, but neither are we ready to enter heaven. Such souls are assured of their salvation, but the life of charity has not yet been made perfect in them. The dross of the tendencies and temporal effects associated with sinful choices accumulates and weighs down the soul. What is the fate of the person who has not, through his or her actions, rejected the Lord through unrepentant mortal sin, but who is nonetheless attached to sin in some way at the moment of death?

For such persons God lovingly provides a means to enter his presence. Purgatory is the intermediary state of purification after death in which these souls are cleansed of nonmortal sins, healed, and made ready to see God. Purgatory "does not indicate a place,

---

10. Auer, Ratzinger, *Eschatology: Death and Eternal Life*, 217.

but a condition of existence."[11] This does not mean that God is strict, severe, or cruel, but instead reveals a new dimension of his abiding mercy. God makes them ready so that their joy and happiness on seeing him may be full from its very first moment. These souls are assured of entering heaven, yet that is delayed until they are freed from all obstacles through the grace of God.[12] Freed in such a way, they are as ready as a human being can be to enter the presence of God. Thus purgatory allows divine love to grow in the soul, free from the danger of our committing further sin. The guilt of minor sins, bad habits, and lesser faults is purified in purgatory.

The teaching on purgatory brings together the two great facts of our daily life: the frailty of the human being and the mercy of God. This teaching on final purification after death has strong biblical roots. In the Second Book of Maccabees, we learn that Judas and his companions pray for the dead whom they knew to be attached to sin prior to their death: "They turned to supplication, praying that the sin that had been committed might be wholly blotted out" (2 Mac 12:42). They continue their prayers by taking up a collection that they send to Jerusalem to be used for an expiatory sacrifice in the Temple for the sins of the dead: "Therefore he made atonement for the dead, so that they might be delivered from their sin" (2 Mac 12:45). The Lord Jesus indicates that lesser offenses can be forgiven after death when he tells the Pharisees that some sins will not be forgiven "in the age to come" (Mt 12:32). It would seem from the context and emphasis that some lesser sins can be so forgiven. Jesus underscores with his disciples the need for purification from sin and its effects through an image: ". . . you will be thrown into prison.

---

11. Saint John Paul II, *The Trinity's Embrace*, 236.
12. *Summa Theologiae* Suppl q 69, a 1, a 2.

The Last Things   *157*

Truly I tell you, you will never get out until you have paid the last penny" (Mt 5:26).

Saint Paul tells us that at the judgment "the work of each builder will become visible . . . it will be revealed with fire, and the fire will test what sort of work each has done. If what has been built on the foundation survives, the builder will receive a reward. If the work is burned up, the builder will suffer loss; the builder will be saved, but only as through fire" (1 Cor 3:13–15). The Book of Revelation emphasizes, "But nothing unclean will enter it [heaven]" (Rev 21:27). The Church teaches that we are to intercede for the souls in purgatory by offering up good works, giving alms, praying, and offering Mass for them.[13]

The merits of Christ are the sole, all-sufficient means of salvation offered to every person. The doctrine of purgatory in no way implies that something is lacking in Christ's salvific work. It is quite the opposite. Purgatory is the saving application of the merits of the sacrifice of Christ for the final perfection of those who die in the state of grace, but who still are burdened with the guilt of unresolved faults, imperfections, and lesser sins that remain at the moment of death.[14] The fire of purification in purgatory is completely different from the punishments of hell. Saint Catherine of Genoa, the sixteenth-century mystic, wrote a thorough reflection on purgatory in her work *Purgation and Purgatory*. She reminds us that the souls who enter purgatory are faithful souls. They still retain some of the "rust and stain" of sin,[15] but the rust is worn away in purgatory. She also describes a type of joy in purgatory. The soul is

---

13. See *DS* 1580; 1820, and also Pope Benedict XVI, *Spe Salvi*, 48.
14. See Auer, Ratzinger, *Eschatology: Death and Eternal Life*, 189.
15. Saint Catherine of Genoa, *Purgation and Purgatory*, 71.

joyful because it is in the place in which God wills it to be for now.[16] The souls in purgatory find joy in the will of God and in becoming more open to his will. Yet, this also brings suffering to these souls because their deep desire is for God. The fiery charity of purgatory prepares the souls for the life of heaven.

The teaching on purgatory is more clearly grasped once we understand that sin has at least two major consequences (see *CCC* 1472). The first effect of mortal sin happens immediately when we commit it, destroying our communion here and now with God, our neighbor, and ourselves.

The second effect of mortal sin does not take place right now, today, though it flows from the first effect. If unrepented at the moment of death, mortal sin has the effect of our losing eternal life with God, earning eternal punishment in hell. When mortal sins are sincerely confessed in the sacrament of Penance, the sacrament remits the eternal punishment due to sin, namely, eternal separation from God in hell. However, even when the guilt of mortal sin is forgiven, the temporal consequences of the sin remain. One still must deal with, endure, and bear the effects in this present world of the sin committed. If this purification is not completed in this present life, then it will be finished in purgatory.

The "here-and-now" effect of sin is known as the temporal punishment due to sin. Venial sin burdens and mortal sin breaks our relationship with God, with our brothers and sisters, and with our deepest self. These effects are part of the temporal punishment due to sin. God does not create this punishment or use it as a kind of revenge for sin. The punishment of sin follows immediately upon the nature of sin. For example, if we have lied to someone, they are less likely to

---

16. See Saint Catherine of Genoa, *Purgation and Purgatory*, 77.

trust others, perhaps for a very long time. Similarly, violence begets violence. If we act with anger toward someone else, perhaps someone we do not even know, that anger has an effect on them. The driver we yell at this morning can very easily take that pent up anger home with him and let it out on his wife and children.

Christ has made atonement and satisfaction for all sin. He has endowed the inexhaustible treasury of the Church with the immeasurable riches of his grace. The Church may apply the merits of Christ from this treasury to the remission of the temporal punishment due to sin in the form of indulgences, which are closely connected to the sacrament of Penance. A partial indulgence is the remission of a portion of the temporal punishment, while a plenary indulgence is the remission of all of it. The conditions to receive a plenary indulgence are set by the Church and include detachment from all sin, even venial sin, a pious action such as a pilgrimage or particular devotion, fervent and worthy reception of the sacraments of Penance and the Eucharist, and prayers for the intentions of the Holy Father.[17] Indulgences serve to strengthen the life of virtue and to help us receive the benefits of the merits of Christ. In the solidarity of the communion of saints, the benefits of indulgences can also be applied to those who have already died (see *CCC* 1471).

Blessed John Ruusbroec, the fourteenth-century Flemish mystic, reminds us that praying for the souls in purgatory is a crucial dimension of our spiritual life. Blessed John emphasizes that throughout the day the Holy Spirit himself will inspire us to pray for them in such a way that we know for sure that the inspiration

---

17. Apostolic Penitentiary, *Manual of Indulgences: Norms and Grants* (Washington, D.C.: United States Conference of Catholic Bishops, 2006), 18, N20.1.

comes from the Spirit of God himself.[18] The principal purpose of the funeral Mass is to pray for the repose of the soul of the deceased. Our prayer for the dead is a palpable and effective sign of our bond with them, so that they may more quickly be purified and enter the bliss of heaven.

Heaven

When I was much younger, I believed that if we simply built a supersonic rocket that thrust past the clouds, stars, planets, and, finally, the entire solar system, we would eventually reach heaven. But a vast chasm exists between *the heavens* and heaven. The visible heavens, the seemingly endless atmosphere that stretches above our heads, is a cosmological phenomenon. Heaven, the dwelling of God (see Ps 14:2; 20:7; 53:3), is beyond the reaches of the visible universe. Father John Saward points out that just as the meteorological heavens reach far above our heads, so too God's heaven reaches far above us in the metaphysical sense.[19]

Heaven is the place of God's throne (see Mt 5:34; 23:22). He is not isolated in heaven; on the contrary, he reaches out to us (see Ps 80:15; 102:20; Is 63:15; Lam 3:50). The heavens cannot contain God (see 1 Kgs 8:27; Ps 113:4). In the Old Testament, God comes down (see Gn 11:5; 18:21) to speak to us. His dwelling and commands draw close to us (see Dt 30:11). God promises to rend the heavens and "come down" (Is 64:1). Jesus calls us to share in the Kingdom of Heaven (see Mt 5:20; 7:21; 18:3; 19:23). For the human being,

---

18. See Blessed John Ruusbroec, *The Spiritual Espousals* as in *John Ruusbroec: The Spiritual Espousals and Other Works* in The Classics of Western Spirituality (New Jersey: Paulist Press, 1985), 104–105.

19. See John Saward, *Sweet and Blessed Country*, 17.

heaven is the fullness of communion with God in eternal life, the time we see him face to face (see 1 Jn 3:2) and live with him forever in the happiness of everlasting life. Heaven is the perfect union of love, the perfection of love that satisfies the deepest longing of humanity.[20] The vision and love of God is the fundamental goal of God's plan, which brings infinite joy to the just and fulfills human existence. We begin to encounter Christ during our life on earth in the sacraments, beginning with Baptism, and in the life of the Church. Prayer cries to heaven (see Gn 4:10; Sir 35:17; 1 Mac 3:50; 4:10; 9:46).

Heaven is eternal life with Christ, the unending reward of those who die in the state of God's grace and who have been completely purified. In heaven we encounter the personal reality of the glorified Lord in such a way that Jesus draws us into an utterly unique encounter with the Blessed Trinity. "This perfect life with the Most Holy Trinity—this communion of life and love with the Trinity, with the Virgin Mary, the angels, and all the blessed . . . is the ultimate end and fulfillment of the deepest human longings, the state of supreme, definitive happiness."[21] In heaven, "God totally permeates the whole man with his plenitude."[22] Stunningly, Saint Paul tells us, ". . . no eye has seen, nor ear heard, nor the human heart conceived, what God has prepared for those who love him" (1 Cor 2:9). Those who are received into the life of heaven can never lose it. All the redeemed, of all times and places, because of their union with Christ, unite in the communion of saints.

Jesus promises the just the reward of heaven (see Mt 5:12), and encourages us to store up "treasure in heaven" (Mt 6:20). He

---

20. See Hans Urs von Balthasar, *The Christian State of Life*, 123.

21. *CCC* 1024.

22. Auer, Ratzinger, *Eschatology: Death and Eternal Life*, 235.

tells his faithful followers: "In my Father's house there are many dwelling places. If it were not so, would I have told you that I go to prepare a place for you? And if I go and prepare a place for you, I will come again and will take you to myself, so that where I am, there you may be also" (Jn 14:2–3). Giving to the poor is a path to securing this treasure (see Mt 19:21). "It lies neither inside nor outside the space of our world, even though it must not be detached from the cosmos as some mere 'state.'"[23] Saint Pope John Paul II tells us: "we know that the 'heaven' or 'happiness' in which we will find ourselves is neither an abstraction nor a physical place in the clouds, but a living, personal relationship with the Holy Trinity. It is our meeting with the Father that takes place in the risen Christ through the communion of the Holy Spirit."[24] Heaven is a place, though not a "place" in a way familiar to us.[25] The angels behold the face of God in heaven. So, too, do the souls of human beings; and in heaven they behold forever the clear vision of God in perfect supernatural beatitude. For Blessed Denys, God is in a place not by being bound by it, but by surpassing or transcending it.[26] Thus, God dwells in heaven as the place in which he reveals himself ever more clearly and works ever more magnificently. We cannot see God unless God, through his divine grace and the light of his glory, unites us to himself and gives us the very capacity to receive him.[27]

---

23. Ibid., 237.

24. Saint John Paul II, *The Trinity's Embrace*, 229.

25. *Summa Theologiae* Suppl q 69, a 1, ad 1.

26. See Blessed Denys, *Enarratio in Psalmum 5 poenitentialem*, n. 20 *DCOO* 14. 449B. as in Saward, *Sweet and Blessed Country*, 23.

27. See *CCC* 1028; see also Council of Vienne, *Ad nostrum qui* (1312); *DS* 895; *STh* Ia, q. 12, a. 4; and Hans Urs von Balthasar, *Theodrama II*, 184.

The blessed in heaven enjoy the Beatific Vision, which means seeing God as he is, beholding the vision of the inner life and the infinite perfection of the Blessed Trinity.[28] The Beatific Vision is the full delight of happiness with God. In this magnificent light, that once received can never be lost, the blessed behold the beauty of Christ and the Virgin Mary. Likewise the blessed behold the brilliance of the angelic light. Saint Thomas explains that the blessed in heaven also know what is related to them as persons. They know and converse with each other; they know the states of their loved ones on earth or in purgatory, and the prayers we make for their intercession.[29]

The general judgment and the resurrection of the body

The Church teaches that besides the particular judgment, at the end of time another judgment will take place, called the general judgment. The general judgment will not change the decision of the particular judgment but it will occur at the second coming of Christ, when, as the Prophet Isaiah foretold, God will "tear open the heavens and come down" (Is 64:1). Jesus speaks of "'the Son of Man coming in a cloud' with power and great glory" (Lk 21:27). He likewise tells his disciples, "When the Son of Man comes in his glory, and all the angels with him, then he will sit on the throne of his glory. All the nations will be gathered before him, and he will separate people one from another as a shepherd separates the sheep from

---

28. See the Council of Florence, *Decretum pro Graecis* (1439); *DS* 1300.
29. See *Summa Theologiae* IIIa, q. 10, a. 2 and *4 Sent* d. 45, q. 3 a. 1. See also John Saward, *Sweet and Blessed Country*, 46.

the goats" (Mt 25:31–32). The Book of Revelation describes the moment when Christ returns in glory as the Lord of history: "Look! He is coming with the clouds; every eye will see him" (Rev 1:7).

Some people have attempted to calculate the timing of the end of the world by tracing various prophecies to historical events such as wars, natural disasters, and persecutions (see Mk 13:6–13; 21–23). The Lord himself tells us that only the Father knows the day or the hour: "But about that day or hour no one knows, neither the angels in heaven, nor the Son, but only the Father. Beware, keep alert; for you do not know when the time will come" (Mk 13:32–33). The apostles said clearly, "It is not for you to know the times or periods that the Father has set by his own authority" (Acts 1:7). Rather than attempting to foretell the date of the Second Coming, the Christian lives in constant readiness to meet Christ. This readiness is not an anxious or worried apprehension, but a spirit of daily fidelity and dedicated awareness to the movement of the Holy Spirit. The return of Christ at the general judgment is a moment of inexpressible joy: "God did not send the Son into the world to condemn the world, but in order that the world might be saved through him" (Jn 3:17; see 12:47). We rejoice therefore that the Father has given "all judgment to the Son" (Jn 5:22; see Jn 5:27; Mt 25:31; Acts 10:42; 17:31; 2 Tim 4:1). The judgment of Christ is not alien or harsh; for it reflects our own free decisions: "The one who rejects me and does not receive my word has a judge; on the last day the word that I have spoken will serve as judge" (Jn 12:48).

Sacred Scripture teaches us that God the Father "has put all things under [Christ's] feet" (Eph 1:22). On the last day we are called before the throne and judgment seat of God to give an account of our lives (see Rom 14:10; 2 Cor 5:10). Then Christ will pass a final and definitive judgment on our deeds. This judgment does not change the verdict reached at the particular judgment, but will serve to make known the hearts of all (see Mk 12:38–40; Lk 12:1–3; Mt 25:40). The ultimate meaning of all things throughout all times and places will be revealed in its fullness. As all the powers of the cosmos bow to Christ, the saved will be "irradiated by the light of Christ" whose brilliance "reveals what is hidden in [us]," even things unknown to we ourselves.[30] As the prophet Isaiah said:

> On this mountain the LORD of hosts will make for all peoples
>   a feast of rich food, a feast of well-aged wines,
>   of rich food filled with marrow, of well-aged wines strained clear.
>
> And he will destroy on this mountain
>   the shroud that is cast over all peoples,
>   the sheet that is spread over all nations;
>   he will swallow up death forever.
>
> Then the Lord GOD will wipe away the tears from all faces,
>   and the disgrace of his people he will take away from all the
>   earth,
>   for the LORD has spoken.(Is 25:6–8)

We see by faith on our earthly pilgrimage. At the general judgment we will see God in the fullness of life (see 1 Jn 3:2). And so, Saint Paul can say, "When all things are subjected to him, then the Son himself will also be subjected to the one who put all things in subjection under him, so that God may be all in all" (1 Cor 15:28). Von Balthasar says, "eternal life is not the negation of time and space, but the unimaginable superabundance of times and spaces in which freedom can operate, expressing the fullness of life that is eternally going on in God."[31]

---

30. Hans Urs von Balthasar, *Theodrama II*, 158.
31. Ibid., 279.

The general judgment is also the time of the general resurrection. The Prophet Daniel said: "Many of those who sleep in the dust of the earth shall awake, some to everlasting life, and some to shame and everlasting contempt" (Dn 12:2). The Lord proclaimed: "the hour is coming when all who are in their graves will hear his voice And will come out" (Jn 5:28). Saint Paul likewise emphasizes: "Listen, I will tell you a mystery! We will not all die, but we will all be changed, in a moment, in the twinkling of an eye, at the last trumpet. For the trumpet will sound, and the dead will be raised imperishable, and we will be changed" (1 Cor 15:51–52). At this moment, God becomes all in all (see 1 Cor 15:18). The Book of Revelation describes the judgment:

> Then I saw a great white throne and the one who sat on it; the earth and the heaven fled from his presence, and no place was found for them. And I saw the dead, great and small, standing before the throne, and books were opened. Also another book was opened, the book of life. And the dead were judged according to their works, as recorded in the books. And the sea gave up the dead that were in it, Death and Hades gave up the dead that were in them, and all were judged according to what they had done. (Rev 20:11–13)

At the general judgment, based on the resurrection of Christ, the bodies of all who have ever lived will be raised, the good to eternal life and the evil to damnation. Because the soul's very essence is to be the form of the body, the soul is forever ordered to matter in some way.[32] At the general resurrection the separated souls in heaven, purgatory, or hell will be reunited with their bodies. For those who are saved, glory will flow from their souls into their

---

32. See Auer, Ratzinger, *Eschatology: Death and Eternal Life*, 179.

bodies and mark the resurrection of the whole person.[33] Saint Paul also asks the question, so as to lead us further into the mystery: "How are the dead raised? With what kind of body do they come?" (1 Cor 15:35). Natural science cannot explain the nature of the resurrection of the body. The resurrection of the body and eternal life go beyond reason, but do not contradict it. The teaching of the Church leads us to understand that in the resurrection of the body matter belongs to the spirit in a completely new and definitive way.[34] The resurrected body will be completely subject to the soul. As such, the body will show forth the brilliant clarity of the blessed soul. The person can never suffer or die.[35] The blessed in heaven who until that point have experienced the light of glory in their souls, will from then on enjoy the perfect happiness of heaven in a more complete way as they experience it in their bodies as well.[36]

The Second Book of Maccabees includes the account of a mother and seven brothers who refuse to betray the laws of God, even though they endure torture. As the third brother is brought forward to be mistreated, he is told to stretch out his hands so that his torturers may cut them off. The brother boldly does so, and says, "I got these from heaven, and because of his laws I disdain them, and from him I hope to get them back again" (2 Mac 7:11). Even though our physical remains decay and become part of the universe, they are never destroyed completely, they will be transformed. Saint Paul

---

33. See Sacred Congregation for the Doctrine of the Faith, *Letter on Certain Questions Concerning Eschatology* May 17, 1979: *AAS* 71 (1979), 941 see also, Saint Thomas, *4 Sent.* d. 44 q.2 a. 4a.

34. See Auer, Ratzinger, *Eschatology: Death and Eternal Life*, 192, 194.

35. See John Saward, *Sweet and Blessed Country*, 35.

36. See *Summa Theologiae* Ia IIae q 4, a 5 ad 4 and 5; see also John Saward, *Sweet and Blessed Country*, 36–37.

teaches that the entire creation "will be set free from its bondage to decay and will obtain the freedom of the glory of the children of God" (Rom 8:21). Paul Claudel tells us that no matter how far our bodies decay into dust, they cannot escape the record God keeps of them; they hold the promise of resurrection.[37] The Prophet Isaiah proclaims: "Your dead shall live, their corpses shall rise. O dwellers in the dust, awake and sing for joy! For your dew is a radiant dew, and the earth will give birth to those long dead" (Is 26:19). Saint Paul makes clear the astounding truth: "we are expecting a Savior, the Lord Jesus Christ. He will transform the body of our humiliation that it may be conformed to the body of his glory, by the power that also enables him to make all things subject to himself" (Phil 3:20–21). The resurrection presupposes a profoundly different kind of matter, a transformed cosmos that is beyond all we can conceive.[38] In time and space, the body is made of countless cells, corpuscles, and molecules that die over time and are replaced by new ones in the cycle of growth. These individual pieces do not all add up to the being that is me. Saint Thomas explains that "whatever goes with the nature of a human body was entirely in the body of Christ when he rose again." For Saint Thomas this includes "flesh, bones, blood, and other such things, [as] are of the very nature of the human body."[39] All of these things are in Christ's body with integrity. Saint Thomas asserts that "all the particles which belong to the truth and integrity of human nature are present in the resurrected body."[40] "Even the hairs on your head are all counted" (Mt 10:30; see Lk 21:18). Our bodies hold no secrets from the Creator

---

37. See Paul Claudel, *I Believe in God: A Meditation on the Apostles' Creed*, 272.
38. See Auer, Ratzinger, *Eschatology: Death and Eternal Life*, 106.
39. *Summa Theologiae* IIIa, q 54, a 3.
40. *Summa Theologiae* IIIa, q 54, a 3, ad 3.

(see Ps 139:15). "For this perishable body must put on imperishability, and this mortal body must put on immortality" (1 Cor 15:53). We are recreated entirely into a new life, over which death no longer has any claim whatsoever.

> In a magnificent blaze of energy, eternally released from the claims of entropy, the world will thus enter into Christ's personal glory; Christ will permeate it with a life that has shaken off the servitude of death and will make it . . . the new mankind of the Resurrection. Making his way into the furthest recesses of every galaxy and every atom, and *reversing* for ever and ever the structures of death so that they become structures of life, the Christ of the Resurrection will himself appear. . . .[41]

Pope Benedict XVI, writing as Joseph Ratzinger explains that "by announcing a new heaven and a new earth, the Bible makes it clear that the whole of creation is destined to become the vessel of God's Glory. All of created reality is to be drawn into blessedness."[42]

The souls of the just in heaven will experience even further joy at the general judgment. Until then they will have enjoyed the happiness of heaven as a separated soul. At the general judgment they will enjoy the happiness of heaven in a new way as both body and soul are reunited. Those who are in hell will likewise experience increased torment, for then they will experience eternal separation from God not simply as a separated soul, but also in the body.[43]

---

41. Gustave Martelet, *The Risen Christ and the Eucharistic World*, 79.

42. Auer, Ratzinger, *Eschatology: Death and Eternal Life*, 237; see also, *The Church's Confession of Faith*, 172.

43. See *Summa Theologiae* Suppl q 69, a 1, ad 4.

Conclusion

A long line of people stretched out the front door of the large house, across the porch, and down the front steps. It was the same funeral home. The sterile features hadn't changed. I passed the same overly polished podium, turned the same corner, and now stood in the exact same position I had stood in sixteen years earlier. A coffin was propped open in the exact same place. Several things were different, however. It wasn't a warm August afternoon in 1977, but a cold mid-October morning in 1993. I hadn't stood in the line. I had arrived early and walked right in. It wasn't a friend's father who was lying in the coffin. It was my father.

He had died somewhat suddenly. I had been home on break from school over the Columbus Day weekend. I awoke that Monday and heard him groaning in terrible pain. We later learned that he had a ruptured aortic aneurism, a tear in his heart. The emergency room doctor told us that once the pain begins, the person has less than a ten percent chance of survival. My father died in surgery.

Now I stood in the exact same place I had stood sixteen years before . . . when, at seven years old, I first saw a dead body. Now I stood there by myself. At the funeral home, as the line of friends diminished, I stepped to one side. My family and friends were close by, a few feet away in the parlor of the funeral home. They were conversing, expressing condolences to one another. The moment was mine alone. As I stood there next to the coffin, looking in, I saw again that blunt contrast of a dark suit against satin white pillows. I wondered, again, why the pillows were there. I stood in the exact place where my legs went solid, my breath hid in my lungs, and I stared overwhelmed and open mouthed at the body of my friend's father. As it had been years ago, my breath was still a coward and my legs found it just as easy to freeze in place.

I also felt the same curious urge to touch my father's hands. I felt an initial burst of fear but almost immediately realized that with these same hands my father had thrown the baseball to me in the backyard. They were the same hands that he had clasped over mine to show me how to hold and swing a baseball bat. They were the same hands that had turned the pages of storybooks as he read to me. I still remember him reading the familiar Christmas stories on my bedroom floor on Christmas Eve. His were the hands that had guided me along at the funeral home so long ago. His hand was still guiding me.

I reached out and touched his right hand. This time I didn't yank my hand back. The old fear came fluttering from the walls of my stomach, but not for long. Instead, though my father's skin felt unusual, unfamiliar, and rough, *he would never hurt me*. I kept my hand on his.

In touching his hand I did not simply *touch* the mystery; I *felt* the mystery. My father had been through the ultimate mystery, the passage from death to life. I perceived, experienced, and uncovered a deeply rooted certitude, a new movement in my soul. This unpredictable and surprising awareness now shed an original light on everything I have ever heard in Sacred Scripture about Christ conquering death. It all came quietly and convincingly alive for me in that moment in a way I could never explain with mere words. Saint Augustine asks, "Why does our human frailty hesitate to believe that mankind will one day live with God?"[1] As I stood by my father's body that day all my hesitation evaporated.

Every theological truth I read or learned before or since about death and resurrection stood out as verified on a level beyond the academic, theoretical, or demonstrable. My father, clinging to Christ, had stepped into and passed through the chaos of death. *He had met death.* He had been baptized as an infant, received the sacraments, especially final absolution in the emergency room on the day he was dying. He had clung to Christ. Having conquered death, Jesus transformed it. Jesus is risen. My father had stepped into death and had, therefore, joined himself even further to Christ. Yet, my father's body lay still before me. In that brief moment, *presence and absence collided* for me. The absence brought about by the death of the man who had always been there, even in the most difficult of times; the newly felt unfathomable absence of the man who had brought me into being ... and, yet, the *presence* of his physical body.

My father's presence and his body had always been so familiar to me. This very familiar body that lay before me in the funeral home was now a mystery to me, but a mystery I could touch and feel. In fact, his physical body was more than a mystery; it had been transformed into a *sign* that had both begun and at the same time, was now awaiting final transformation in Christ.

The sign is this: in the mystery of divine love, what had taken place in Christ was now to take place in my father. The Second Vatican Council teaches that death has a paschal character.[2] Even my father's dead body pointed now to Christ ... for me it did so in

---

1. Saint Augustine, *Sermo Guelferbytanus* 3: PLS 2, 545–546.
2. See Second Vatican Council, *Sacrosanctum Concilium*, 81.

a personal way. The words of Saint John capture the perception: "We declare to you what was from the beginning, what we have heard, what we have seen with our eyes, what we have looked at and touched with our hands, concerning the word of life" (1 Jn 1:1).

My father's body pointed to the living Clue, Jesus Christ. And so, I continue to faithfully follow the thread. The living Thread is Jesus Christ who invites us all into the mysterious immensity of his Church. In his Church we journey. We move from a promise to its fulfillment in the unforeseeable action of God, and step into the inner and eternal meaning of the Lord's cross and resurrection. And we are summoned to take that last step, to await another line, what we pray will be a long line. And we pray that this line stretches not from a funeral home, but an eternal mansion, one of many:

> "In my Father's house there are many dwelling places. If it were not so, would I have told you that I go to prepare a place for you? And if I go and prepare a place for you, I will come again and will take you to myself, so that where I am, there you may be also. And you know the way to the place where I am going." Thomas said to him, "Lord, we do not know where you are going. How can we know the way?" Jesus said to him, "I am the way, and the truth, and the life. No one comes to the Father except through me." (Jn 14:2–6)

As we await that immeasurable moment, we take as our prayer Saint Augustine's words in the remarkable ending of the *City of God*:

> After this period God shall rest as on the seventh day, when he shall give us (who shall be the seventh day) rest in himself. But there is not now space to treat of these ages; suffice it to say that the seventh shall be our Sabbath, which shall be brought to a close, not by an evening, but by the Lord's day, as an eighth and eternal day, consecrated by the resurrection of Christ, and prefiguring the eternal repose not only of the spirit, but also of

the body. There we shall rest and see, see and love, love and praise. This is what shall be in the end without end. For what other end do we propose to ourselves than to attain to the kingdom of which there is no end?[3]

---

3. Saint Augustine, *The City of God*, trans. by J. F. Shaw, Nicene and Post-Nicene Fathers, First Series, Volume Two (Christian Literature Publishing Company, 1887), 511. Bk XXII; Ch XXX.

Selected Bibliography

Aquinas, Thomas. *Summa Theologiae*. In *Basic Writings of St. Thomas Aquinas*. Edited by Anton C. Pegis. New York: Random House, 1945.

Augustine. *The City of God*. Translated by J. F. Shaw. *Nicene and Post-Nicene Fathers*, First Series, Volume Two. Christian Literature Publishing Company, 1887.

_____.*Confessions*. Text and commentary by James J. O'Donnell. http://www.stoa.org/hippo/.

_____. *Tractates on the Gospel of John*. Edited by P. Schaff, et al. *A Select Library of the Nicene and Post-Nicene Fathers of the Christian Church*. Michigan: Eerdmans, 1994.

Balthasar, Hans Urs von. *The Christian State of Life*. San Francisco: Ignatius Press, 2002.

_____. *Explorations in Theology V: Man Is Created*. San Francisco: Ignatius Press, 2014.

_____. *The Glory of the Lord: A Theological Aesthetics I: Seeing the Form*. San Francisco: Ignatius Press, 1982.

_____. *The Glory of the Lord: A Theological Aesthetics II: Studies in Theological Style: Clerical Styles*. San Francisco: Ignatius Press, 1984.

_____. *The Glory of the Lord: A Theological Aesthetics VI: Theology: The Old Covenant.* San Francisco: Ignatius Press, 1991.

_____. *The Glory of the Lord: A Theological Aesthetics VII: Theology: The New Covenant.* San Francisco: Ignatius Press, 1989.

_____. *Theodrama: Theological Dramatic Theory I: Prologomena.* San Francisco: Ignatius Press, 1988.

_____. *Theodrama: Theological Dramatic Theory II: Dramatis Personae: Man in God.* San Francisco: Ignatius Press, 1990.

_____. *Theodrama: Theological Dramatic Theory III: Dramatis Personae: Persons in Christ.* San Francisco: Ignatius Press, 1993.

_____. *Theodrama: Theological Dramatic Theory IV: The Action.* San Francisco: Ignatius Press, 1994.

_____. *Theodrama: Theological Dramatic Theory V: The Last Act.* San Francisco: Ignatius Press, 2003.

_____. *Theologic I: Truth of the World.* San Francisco: Ignatius Press, 2000.

_____. *Theologic III: The Spirit of Truth.* San Francisco: Ignatius Press, 2005.

_____. *A Theology of History.* San Francisco: Ignatius Press, 1994.

_____. *Unless You Become Like This Child.* San Francisco: Ignatius Press, 1991.

Bérulle, Pierre de. *Discourse on the State* and *the Grandeurs of Jesus.* Edited by William Thompson. In *Bérulle and the French School: Selected Writings*, The Classics of Western Spirituality. Mahway, NJ: Paulist Press, 1989.

Bouillard, Henri. *The Logic of the Faith.* New York: Sheed and Ward, 1967.

Bouyer, Louis. *The Meaning of the Monastic Life.* New York: P. J. Kennedy and Sons, 1955.

_____. *The Spirituality of the New Testament and the Fathers.* New York: Desclee Company, 1960.

Bunge, Gabriel. *Dragon's Wine and Angel's Bread: The Teaching of Evagrius Ponticus on Anger and Meekness.* New York: St. Vladimir's Seminary Press, 2009.

Catherine of Genoa. *Purgation and Purgatory.* In *Catherine of Genoa, Purgation and Purgatory, The Spiritual Dialogue.* The Classics of Western Spirituality. Mahwah, NJ: Paulist Press, 1979.

Chrysologos, Peter. *Sermon 63.* Edited by E. Barnecut. In *Journey with the Fathers: Commentaries on the Sunday Gospels Year A.* New York: New City Press, 1992.

Cicero, Marcus Tullius. *Letters to Atticus,* VII, 18, 1. Translated by E. O. Winstedt. New York: MacMillan, 1913.

Claudel, Paul. *I Believe in God: A Meditation on the Apostles' Creed.* San Francisco: Ignatius Press, 2002.

Cyril of Alexandria, *Commentary on Luke.* Translated by R. Payne Smith. New York: Studion Publishers, 1983.

Daniélou, Jean. *The Angels and Their Mission: According to the Fathers of the Church.* Translated by David Heimann. Westminster, MD: Newman Press, 1957.

_____. *Holy Pagans of the Old Testament.* Translated by Felix Faber. New York: Longman's, Green, and Co., 1956.

Dubay, Thomas. *The Evidential Power of Beauty: Science and Theology Meet.* San Francisco: Ignatius Press, 1999.

Dulles, Avery. "The Population of Hell." In *First Things,* May 2003.

Emonet, Pierre-Marie. *The Dearest Freshness Deep Down Things: An Introduction to the Philosophy of Being.* New York: Crossroad, 1999.

Féret, H. M. *The Apocalypse of St. John.* Maryland: The Newman Press, 1958.

Gladwell, Malcolm. *David and Goliath: Underdogs, Misfits, and the Art of Battling Giants.* New York: Little, Brown, and Company, 2013.

Grech, Prosper. *Acts of the Apostles Explained: A Doctrinal Commentary* New York: Alba House, 1966.

Gregory the Great. *Pastoral Care.* Translated by Henry Davis. New Jersey: Paulist Press, 1950.

Hugh of Balma, *The Roads to Zion Mourn.* Translated by Dennis Martin. In *Carthusian Spirituality: The Writings of Hugh of Balma and Guigo de Ponte.* Classics of Western Spirituality Series. Mahwah, NJ: Paulist Press, 1997.

Ignatius of Antioch, *Letter to the Ephesians*. In *The Apostolic Fathers*. Translated by J. B Lightfoot New York: Macmillan, 1891.

Kreeft, Peter. *Socratic Logic: A Logic Text Using Socratic Method, Platonic Questions, and Aristotelian Principles.* Indiana: St. Augustine's Press, 2004.

Ladaria, Luis. "Humanity in the Light of Christ in the Second Vatican Council." In *Vatican II: Assessment and Perspectives, Volume II*. Edited by Rene Latourelle. New Jersey: Paulist Press, 1989.

Leiva-Merikakis, Erasmo. *Love's Sacred Order: The Four Loves Revisited.* San Francisco: Ignatius Press, 2000.

Léon-Dufour, Xavier. *Resurrection and the Message of Easter.* New York: Holt, Rinehart, and Winston, 1975.

Lubac, Henri de. *A Brief Catechesis on Nature and Grace.* San Francisco: Ignatius Press, 1984.

_____. *The Drama of Atheist Humanism.* San Francisco: Ignatius Press, 1995.

Martelet, Gustave. *The Risen Christ and the Eucharistic World.* New Jersey: Seabury Press, 1977.

Maximinus of Trier. *Sermon 14.* In *Corpus Christianorum,* Series Latina. Belgium: Turnhout, 1953.

Nouwen, Henri. *A Letter of Consolation.* New York: Harper Collins, 1982.

Plato. *Timaeus.* Translated by Benjamin Jowett. http://classics.mit.edu/Plato/timaeus.html.

Porphyry the Phoenician. *Isagoge.* Translation, introduction, and notes by E. W. Warren. Toronto: The Pontifical Institute of Mediaeval Studies, 1979.

Ratzinger, Joseph, and Johann Auer. *Eschatology: Death and Eternal Life* Washington, D.C.: The Catholic University of America Press, 1989.

Ratzinger, Joseph. *"In the Beginning . . ." A Catholic Understanding of the Story of Creation and the Fall.* Michigan: Eerdmans, 1995.

Ruusbroec, John. "The Spiritual Espousals." In *John Ruusbroec: The Spiritual Espousals and Other Works.* The Classics of Western Spirituality. Mahway, NJ: Paulist Press, 1985.

Saward, John. *Sweet and Blessed Country: The Christian Hope for Heaven.* Oxford, UK: Oxford University Press, 2008.

Scruton, Roger. *The Face of God.* New York: Continuum, 2012.

Sicard, Damien. "Christian Death." In *The Church at Prayer Volume III: The Sacraments.* Minnesota: The Liturgical Press, 1988.

Speyr, Adrienne von. *John: The Discourses of Controversy, Meditations on John 6–12.* Translated by Brian McNeil. San Francisco: Ignatius Press, 1993.

_____. *Mark: Meditations on the Gospel of Mark.* Translated by Michelle Borras. San Francisco: Ignatius Press, 2012.

Stein, Edith. *The Science of the Cross.* Washington D.C.: ICS Publications, 2002.

Tartt, Donna. *The Goldfinch.* New York: Little, Brown, and Company, 2013.

Theodore the Studite. *Oratio in Adorationem Crucis. PG* 99, 691–694; 698–699.

Vitz, Paul C. *Faith of the Fatherless: The Psychology of Atheism.* Dallas: Spence Publishing Company, 1999.

Wolterstorff, Nicholas. *Lament for a Son.* Michigan: Eerdmans, 1987.

Zellini, Paolo. *A Brief History of Infinity.* Translated by David Marsh. New York: Penguin Books, 2005.

Vatican II

Second Vatican Council. *Gaudium et Spes.* Boston: Pauline Books & Media, 1965.

Second Vatican Council. *Lumen Gentium.* Boston: Pauline Books & Media, 1964.

Second Vatican Council. *Sacrosanctum Concilium.* Boston: Pauline Books & Media, 1964.

Papal Teachings

Benedict XVI. *Jesus of Nazareth: Holy Week: From the Entrance into Jerusalem to the Resurrection.* San Francisco: Ignatius Press, 2011.

_____. *Spe Salvi.* Boston: Pauline Books & Media, 2007.

Francis. *Lumen Fidei.* Boston: Pauline Books & Media, 2013.

John Paul II. *Dives in Misericordia.* Boston: Pauline Books & Media, 1980.

_____. *Dominum et Vivificantem.* Boston: Pauline Books & Media, 1986.

_____. *God, Father and Creator: A Catechesis on the Creed, Volume I.* Boston: Pauline Books & Media, 1996.

_____. *Jesus, Son and Savior: A Catechesis on the Creed, Volume II.* Boston: Pauline Books & Media, 1996.

_____. *Man and Woman He Created Them: A Theology of the Body.* Translated by Michael Waldstein. Boston: Pauline Books & Media, 2006.

_____. *The Trinity's Embrace: God's Saving Plan.* Boston: Pauline Books & Media, 2002.

Other Magisterial Documents

Apostolic Penitentiary, *Manual of Indulgences: Norms and Grants.* Washington, D.C.: United States Conference of Catholic Bishops, 2006.

Catechism of the Catholic Church, Second Edition. Washington, D.C.: United States Conference of Catholic Bishops, 2006.

Sacred Congregation for the Doctrine of the Faith. *Letter on Certain Questions Concerning Eschatology.* May 17, 1979: *AAS* 71 (1979), 941.

The Council of Florence. *Decretum pro Graecis* (1439), *DS* 1300.

ABOUT THE AUTHOR

REVEREND MONSIGNOR J. BRIAN BRANS-FIELD is a priest of the Archdiocese of Philadelphia. He currently serves as the Associate General Secretary of the United States Conference of Catholic Bishops. Msgr. Bransfield received his doctorate in moral theology from the Pontifical John Paul II Institute for Studies on Marriage and Family. Prior to his current appointment, he served as professor of Moral Theology at St. Charles Borromeo Seminary. He is the author of the best-selling books: *The Human Person: According to John Paul II, Living the Beatitudes: A Journey to Life in Christ,* and *Meeting Jesus Christ: Meditations on the Word.*

OTHER TITLES BY
MONSIGNOR J. BRIAN BRANSFIELD

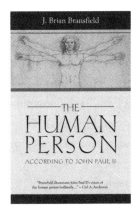

The Human Person:
According to John Paul II

In the twentieth century, three social revolutions—industrial, sexual, and technological—challenged the religious convictions of many. John Paul II's teaching on the Theology of the Body was his response to the resulting societal shifts. J. Brian Bransfield explores John Paul II's reactions to the challenges raised by these revolutions. Within this context, Bransfield then explores how Theology of the Body insights lead us to live the fullness of the Christian life.

Paperback   288 pages
#3394-0 $19.95

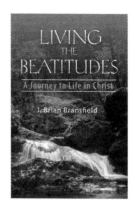

Living the Beatitudes: A Journey to Life in Christ

Are you thirsting for a deeper life-giving relationship with the Lord? The Beatitudes are right before us, if only we would move away from our fears and allow the spirit to guide us. In this book, you are invited to drink from the fountain of holiness and rediscover the mystery of Grace and the peace of living life in the Spirit. Best-selling author J. Brian Bransfield helps you reinvigorate your spirituality by offering a life-giving practice and understanding of the Catholic faith.

Paperback   272 pages
#4544-2 $14.95

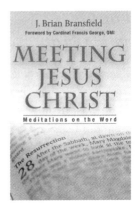

J. Brian Bransfield
Foreword by Cardinal Francis George, OMI

MEETING
JESUS
CHRIST
Meditations on the Word

Meeting Jesus Christ: Meditations on the Word

In this spiritual companion, readers are invited to personally encounter Jesus Christ through twenty-one Scriptural meditations that unlock unique perspectives on the mysteries of his life. J. Brian Bransfield shows us how to develop a more meaningful relationship with Christ through prayer. Each chapter takes up a different Gospel account and draws the reader into meditation. Highlighting the new in the familiar, this guide equips readers with a refreshing way to deepen their prayer life through looking for the unexpected in Scripture. Extending beyond sentimental, this book focuses on Jesus in a way that opens up the mystery and beauty to our everyday lives.

Paperback   256 pages
#4930-8 $15.95

BOOKS & MEDIA

A mission of the Daughters of St. Paul

As apostles of Jesus Christ, evangelizing today's world:

We are CALLED to holiness
by God's living Word and Eucharist.

We COMMUNICATE the Gospel message
through our lives and through all
available forms of media.

We SERVE the Church
by responding to the hopes and needs
of all people with the Word of God,
in the spirit of St. Paul.

For more information visit our Web site: www.pauline.org.

BOOKS & MEDIA

The Daughters of St. Paul operate book and media centers at the following addresses. Visit, call, or write the one nearest you today, or find us at www.pauline.org.

CALIFORNIA

3908 Sepulveda Blvd, Culver City, CA 90230	310-397-8676
935 Brewster Avenue, Redwood City, CA 94063	650-369-4230
5945 Balboa Avenue, San Diego, CA 92111	858-565-9181

FLORIDA

145 S.W. 107th Avenue, Miami, FL 33174	305-559-6715

HAWAII

1143 Bishop Street, Honolulu, HI 96813	808-521-2731

ILLINOIS

172 North Michigan Avenue, Chicago, IL 60601	312-346-4228

LOUISIANA

4403 Veterans Memorial Blvd, Metairie, LA 70006	504-887-7631

MASSACHUSETTS

885 Providence Hwy, Dedham, MA 02026	781-326-5385

MISSOURI

9804 Watson Road, St. Louis, MO 63126	314-965-3512

NEW YORK

64 W. 38th Street, New York, NY 10018	212-754-1110

SOUTH CAROLINA

243 King Street, Charleston, SC 29401	843-577-0175

TEXAS

Currently no book center; for parish exhibits or outreach evangelization, contact: 210-569-0500, or SanAntonio@paulinemedia.com, or P.O. Box 761416, San Antonio, TX 78245

VIRGINIA

1025 King Street, Alexandria, VA 22314	703-549-3806

CANADA

3022 Dufferin Street, Toronto, ON M6B 3T5	416-781-9131

¡También somos su fuente para libros, videos y música en español!